Women of Theresienstadt

Women of Theresienstadt
Voices From a Concentration Camp

RUTH SCHWERTFEGER

BERG
Oxford/New York/Hamburg
Distributed exclusively in the US and Canada by
St Martin's Press, New York

First published in 1989 by
Berg Publishers Limited

77 Morrell Avenue, Oxford OX4 1NQ, UK
175 Fifth Avenue/Room 400, New York, NY 10010, USA
Nordalbingerweg 14, Hamburg 61, FRG

Reprinted 1989

Editorial matter, selection and translations © Berg Publishers Limited 1988

British Library Cataloguing in Publication Data

Women of Theresienstadt: voices from
a concentration camp.
1. Czechoslovakia. Theresienstadt.
Concentration camps. Theresienstadt
concentration camp. Jewish women prisoners,
1941–1944. Biographies. Collections
I. Schwertfeger, Ruth
940.54′72′430922

ISBN 0–85496–192–5

Library of Congress Cataloguing-in-Publication Data

The Women of Theresienstadt: voices from a concentration camp /
edited by Ruth Schwertfeger.
p. cm.
Bibliography: p.
Includes index.
ISBN 0–85496–192–5: $22.00 (est.)
1. Terezín (Czechoslovakia : Concentration camp) 2. Holocaust,
Jewish (1939–1945)—Personal narratives. 3. Women, Jewish-
–Biography. I. Schwertfeger, Ruth.
D805.C9W66 1988
940.54′72′430943—dc19

Printed in Great Britain by Short Run Press Ltd., Exeter

To the memory of my mother Grace Crawford,
and
to my friend Edith Carter who
survived both Theresienstadt and Auschwitz

Lament

Ah, the dead do not die,
Laid out in coffins of the eye,
Invisible. Glaring.

Tears, the homeless
Wrap the day in the
Poorhouse of their heart.
Months.
Years.

Go by.
Do not return.
We have to flee lest words end
And chain our memories in. . . .

Chains melt like wax.

ILSE BLUMENTHAL-WEISS

Contents

Illustrations

Acknowledgements

I would like to acknowledge the contribution of the Yad Vashem in Jerusalem in making available to me most of the memoirs from which I drew my information; special thanks are extended to Hadassah Modlinger. I am also indebted to the Leo Baeck Institute in New York City for permission to use their Theresienstadt memoirs and poems. I would also like to thank the staff of the Terezin Memorial Library and the Prague State Jewish Museum. The Ghetto Fighters' House in Israel, Jim Strong of the Leo Baeck Institute and the Art Museum of Yad Vashem generously allowed me to reproduce examples of art of Theresienstadt. I am grateful to Simon Schuster for permission to quote from *I am a Star: Child of the Holocaust* by Inge Auerbacher, to *Postskriptum* for permission to reproduce poems from *Ohnesarg* by Ilse Blumenthal-Weiss; to the Greenwood Press, Westport, Conn., for permission to quote from *Women in the Resistance and in the Holocaust*, edited by Vera Laska, and to Miriam Merzbacher-Blumenthal for permission to reproduce 'The Lord bless you and keep you'.

Funding to help cover the cost of my research was generously provided by the Milwaukee Jewish Federation and the Wisconsin Society for Jewish Learning. I am grateful to Robert Aronson of the Milwaukee Jewish Federation for believing in my project from the beginning, and to Abraham Peck of the American Jewish Archives, Hebrew Union College, Cincinnati, who provided very helpful information.

At the University of Wisconsin–Milwaukee the Irish poet James Liddy, professor of English, collaborated with me on the translations of the Else Dormitzer poems; his contribution is gratefully acknowledged. I also want to thank Dr Gerhard Rauscher, Chairman of the Department of German for rearranging my teaching schedule to allow time for writing and for his constant support and encouragement. Parts of the manuscript were read at different times by Dr Marcus Bullock and Dr Roswitha Mueller of the German Department, Dr Alan Corré of the Hebrew Department, and Dr Robert Siegel of the English Department. I am grateful for the advice they gave me.

Jeffrey Tackes's technical assistance in the preparation of the manuscript was invaluable. I am also grateful to Ingrid Evenson for her help in typing it.

Ruth Schwertfeger
July 1988

Note on Sources

Full publication or archive details for all memoirs and poems quoted in the text are given in the Bibliography. Page references to printed and paginated sources are given in the footnotes; for unpublished and unfoliated archive material page references are neither possible nor, since these memoirs are usually very short, necessary. The Bibliography titles indicate the language of composition. Translations of memoirs and poems written in German are, unless otherwise indicated, my own.

RS

Introduction

IN the history and literature of the Holocaust the concentration camp at Terezin (or Theresienstadt as the Nazis renamed it) in Czechoslovakia represents two aspects of Nazi terror and genocide as different as they are irreconcilable. On the one hand there is the stark truth of the camp's purpose as an assembly point for the extermination camps of the East; on the other is the Nazi propaganda about it as a model ghetto, a re-settlement oasis in the Protectorate, magnanimously donated by Hitler to European Jews. The hideous reality behind this latter claim has long since been exposed, perhaps most poignantly by the children's art that survived Theresienstadt.[1] Joseph Bor's novel *The Terezin Requiem* has added a new dimension to our understanding of the coexistence of culture and brutality; his depiction of starving Jews singing Verdi's Requiem is among the most grotesque ironies of Holocaust literature. Music and art in Theresienstadt have been the subject of at least two books in English, by Joseph Karas and Gerald Green, contributing significantly to our general knowledge of the camp.

Apart from specific studies such as these, surprisingly little has been written about Theresienstadt, and of what there is most is in German. For this reason perhaps the name Theresienstadt conveys little to the average English-speaking reader. H. G. Adler has written the most comprehensive history of the camp to date; himself one of its survivors, he is considered the most reliable and accurate expert on its history. Another survivor, Zdenek Lederer, has written a thoroughly readable, though less detailed, book than Adler's. I am indebted to both texts for the wealth of information and the statistics they provide, but they both have shortcomings with regard to the literary legacy of the camp.

The ambiguity that surrounded the identity of Theresienstadt—concentration camp versus resettlement town—is probably one reason why it has received little attention in its own right. It has been called 'the strangest of all concentration camps',[2] and 'that strange mongrel, a hybrid of a concentration camp and a ghetto'.[3]

1. See *I Never Saw Another Butterfly*, ed. H. Volavkova.
2. *Terezin*, ed. Frantisek Ehrmann, Otta Heitlinger and Rudolf Iltis, p. 66.
3. *Women in the Resistance and in the Holocaust*, ed. Vera Laska, p. 229.

Another writer says 'If Auschwitz was hell, Theresienstadt was the anteroom'.[4] It was in fact this very ambiguity that generated more terror than death itself and made the word 'anxiety' synonymous with TRANSPORT, which could have been written above the slogan 'Arbeit macht frei' at the entrance.

> The whole life of Terezin was constantly haunted by the spectre of transports to the East, to the unknown, which meant the immediate danger of death. No one knew when his turn would come, where he would go, when, why and with whom. The transports were the ominous culmination of the provisional life in Terezin, they were the harbingers of the next stage on the way to the 'final solution to the Jewish problem'.[5]

The Germans called the processing area for arrival and departure 'die Schleuse' (the sluice). People quickly realized that they were indeed caught in a flood-gate and that the level could be changed at any moment. Fear of the transports was the central anxiety around which all life in Theresienstadt revolved and was at the same time the force that engendered the most impassioned response to impermanence in works of art—literary, musical and visual—that have survived much longer than Theresienstadt's three-and-a-half-year history.

A Czech writer said in 1964: 'We believe that neither film artists, nor writers, poets, sculptors, painters and composers have yet said their last word on the subject that offers itself with such urgency as the theme of the "Terezin ghetto". . . .'[6] Indeed the *first* word has scarcely been said in some areas, and nowhere more faintly than in literature. The neglect of Theresienstadt as a subject of fiction has been noted by Susan Cernyak-Spatz, a Holocaust scholar and a Theresienstadt survivor.

> Another aspect of the Holocaust that has never been touched on by German literary circles is the unique institution Theresienstadt. This little eighteenth century walled town, close to the German–Czech border, was used by the Nazis as a Potemkin village. Neither all ghetto nor all KZ, it was a carefully arranged stage set of a 'protected' Jewish town. This set could be unveiled, whenever the pressures from humanitarian international organizations became too strong and inspection demands could not be

4. *Terezin*, ed. Ehrmann, Heitlinger and Iltis, p. 217.
5. Ibid., p. 136.
6. Ibid.

avoided. It had all the appearances of a central European small town: the obligatory coffee-house, concerts, theater, park, etc., down to stores and a bank. The stores and the bank were dummy fronts and the coffee-house was peopled at certain hours of the day by command. For the cursory inspection, however, it presented all the aspects of a carefree little town, not even remotely resembling the images of the horror-propaganda spread among the Allies about the camps. The reverse of the coin was disease, starvation and hard labor, only somewhat mitigated by the efforts of the Judenrat to maintain at least the spiritual welfare of the inhabitants.[7]

The exception to this neglect is the work of the Czech writer Arnold Lustig whose novels on Terezin have been translated as *Diamonds in the Night* and *Night and Hope*. This lack of literary scholarship becomes even more surprising when one considers the extent to which literary activities flourished during the camp's history (November 1941–May 1945). Adler points out that when in 1944 there was a poetry competition in Theresienstadt, of the 37,000 current inmates 3000 submitted poems.[8] And that was only in German. Adler chooses two male poets—Georg Kafka (a distant relative of Franz Kafka) and Hans Kolben—as representative Theresienstadt poets and tacks on one woman poet—Ilse Weber— to represent the thematic content of all the poetry, written by men and women. He summarily dismisses their quality as 'Reimkrankheit' ('rhyming sickness') and the style of Ilse Weber as 'irritatingly clumsy'.[9] Though this book is not concerned with the rights and wrongs of Adler's viewpoint I hope that this much needed correction will be an outcome.

A recent German publication by Ulrike Migdal closely follows Adler's dismissive attitude towards the serious poetry of Theresienstadt, claims that it lacks objectivity and abstract qualities, concentrates on the same two male poets as Adler, and rationalizes the absence of creativity with the contention that under such conditions it was impossible to write for 'eternity'.[10] Inherent in this argument is the assumption that certain subjects or even settings are more appropriate than others for poetry and posterity, a notion that has persisted beyond the 1940s and spawned comments such as Adorno's, that question the very validity of writing poetry after

7. *German Holocaust Literature*, p. 71.
8. *Theresienstadt 1941–1945*, p. 618.
9. Ibid.
10. *Und die Musik spielt dazu*, p. 23.

Auschwitz.[11] Frieda Aaron's comments on the aesthetic form of Holocaust poetry are also pertinent to Theresienstadt.

> Warnings that there are inherent dangers in transcribing the horrors of the Holocaust into artistic representations would probably astonish most of the writers in the Holocaust. Was it not Chaim Kaplan who said in the Warsaw Ghetto that 'more than bread we need poetry at a time when we don't seem to need it at all'? It was certainly Kaplan who wrote in his *Warsaw Diary* that 'a poet who clothes adversity in poetic form immortalizes it in an everlasting monument'. It is doubtful that either Kaplan or the poets on whom he calls were concerned with problems of aesthetic form.[12]

In his book *The Destruction of the Dutch Jews* Jacob Presser refers to a statement made by Rabbi Dr Leo Baeck, one of Theresienstadt's most famous survivors, that is particularly helpful in establishing a larger framework in which to introduce this book. According to Baeck three things were typical of Theresienstadt.

> The first was that it deliberately created conditions under which life could not flourish: 'Living space was replaced by dying space.' Secondly, it brought out all the worst in people, as more and more of them were squashed together in less and less space. And thirdly, by indiscriminately herding together disparate groups from every part of Europe, it accentuated the tension even further. Theresienstadt was a ghetto, but it was more than that. It was one of the portals to Auschwitz, one of the sluices on the way to the gas-chamber.[13]

The aim of this book is twofold: first, to introduce memoirs and poems, most of them translated into English for the first time, written by women either during their internment or after their release, and second, to explore what Baeck calls Theresienstadt's 'dying space'. The memoirs show that dying space also generated living space. 'Indiscriminate herding together', though it may have generated tension, also promoted a solidarity and bonding, manifesting itself both in spiritual and in gender-specific responses. The former was sometimes expressed in Zionist terms by men and

11. T. W. Adorno, 'Engagement'.
12. 'Poetry in the Holocaust', p. 13.
13. *The Destruction of the Dutch Jews*, p. 530.

women actively involved in focusing hope beyond the parameters of the camp to Erez Israel. David Roskies makes an interesting general comment that also is applicable to Theresienstadt.

Inside the Nazi ghetto, the walls and barbed wire that were to separate the Jews from the surrounding population were also to bring some of the internal boundaries down. The élite were brought closer to the masses, the assimilated closer to the committed, the secular closer to the religious, Yiddish closer to Hebrew. The modernists became, despite their long battles against it, part of the literature of consolation. With the ghetto's intellectuals moving closer to the people, the writers could use the polylingualism of Jewish eastern Europe to restore conceptually and socially the idea of a Jewish nation that was the penultimate consolation for the ultimate destruction.[14]

The idea of making a collection of women's writings from Theresienstadt originally presented itself in the discovery of a slim volume of poems entitled *Theresienstädter Bilder*, written by a survivor of Theresienstadt named Else Dormitzer, and published after her release. This led to inquiries at the major Holocaust archives regarding other women writers and poets, followed in the summer of 1987 by visits to the archives of Yad Vashem in Israel, the Prague State Jewish Museum and, finally, the Terezin Memorial Library. At the Yad Vashem I found further evidence of Dormitzer's considerable contribution to the legacy of Theresienstadt in the form of memoirs which carefully document the last two years of the camp's history. Along with her poems they provided the basic material for this book. A second discovery in the course of my research was the work of Ilse Blumenthal-Weiss, another survivor of Theresienstadt. Several poems taken from her volume *Ohnesarg* are used in Chapter 5.

On a certain level it is hard to separate the issue of women's experiences from the overall reality of camp life. Suffering obliterates gender distinctions and accounts for a certain similarity and levelling of response, particularly apparent in the memoirs. This is not, however, to deny or in any way minimize the existence of a community of women that had distinct parameters. Marlene Heinemann's general observation on gender differences in camp experiences holds true for Theresienstadt: 'Even the most impartial and sensitive male survivor will be unable to provide an outsider's picture of women's experiences in the Nazi camps, since male and

14. *Against the Apocalypse*, p. 196.

female prisoners were segregated in separate camps.'[15] Separation of the sexes in Theresienstadt occurred on arrival but was normally confined to segregation into barracks for sleeping quarters, or sometimes into separate rooms within the same barrack. The main body of this book deals with the specific issues and themes of this community of women and relates the three-and-a-half year history of the camp through their narratives and poems. The first chapter gives a brief historical account of Theresienstadt, drawn largely from Adler and other sources, to serve as background to the memoirs themselves. This is not of course to suggest that the memoirs and poems are factually unreliable; there is remarkable agreement on points of fact and detail among all the surviving material relating to Theresienstadt.

Holocaust memoirs have not on the whole provoked the same degree of polemicizing as has poetry. The issue of reliability has, however, been raised, specifically with regard to the time when memoirs were written. Heinemann holds the view that memoirs written twenty-five or thirty years after the event are likely to lack colour and precision,[16] while Aaron finds that Holocaust writings seem to be remarkably unmodified by the process of time.[17] This latter viewpoint seems to me to be valid for the Theresienstadt memoirs. They have a wide range of composition dates, covering the period of internment, the time immediately after release and thereafter all the way down to the mid-seventies and early eighties. For the most part they share certain characteristics, such as obsession with precise detail (the number of bedbugs killed in a night, the measurement of margarine, the number of pieces of lavatory paper distributed), the same selection of key events of the internment such as the day of the census and the disposal of the urns. Fear of the transports pervades every single memoir. There are also striking omissions: sparse physical descriptions of individuals, who are adumbrated with adjectives such as 'pale' or 'delicate', resulting in a montage-effect of shadows. Sometimes a memory of a woman's former life invades time-present, caused either by a sensory impact, a 'Proustian revelation' that catapults her back in time, or else by an involuntary, sudden and overwhelming sense of loss. Most memoirs end after the liberation, though there are exceptions, such as the account by Margareta Glas-Larsson whose recollections of her experiences are strikingly vivid and detailed.

15. *Gender and Destiny*, p. 3.
16. Ibid., p. 130.
17. 'Poetry in the Holocaust', p. 2.

Aaron sees the practice of daydreaming and reminiscing in the concentration camp as part of the creative process that led to the composition of poems and songs. She writes: 'In doing this, [the women] were immortalizing and sanctifying the past and at the same time, creating oral epithets for fugitive tombstones.'[18] The Theresienstadt memoirs, though, tend to focus more on the present and future, and the past is spoken of in terms of a sudden invasion of present consciousness.

The reasons the women give for recording their experiences cover a wide range. Dormitzer ends her memoir 'Die Kristallnacht' on the rather didactic note that the Germans were both actively and passively involved in the experiences she has narrated and that sympathy with the 'innocent population' is therefore inappropriate. Klara Caro's reasons for recording her experiences are couched in strong, spiritual language and specifically addressed to a Jewish audience with the reminder that the celebration of the strength of the Jewish people should in no way diminish the bestiality of the Nazis.

[My writings] are to show to those who were spared that there are forces, or rather a force, that is stronger than privation or death, more powerful than all the evil that cruelty and satanic sadism can ever devise or practise.

I want to tell the heroic epic in this little book of 'Nevertheless' and 'Despite Everything' and proclaim to the indifferent and the unawakened the story of that spiritual strength which is still alive even in the most difficult times, alive in our martyred, Jewish people, that strength, that Maccabean spirit which the Psalmist celebrates: 'Lau Wechajil, Welau Wechauach.' Not raw, brute strength but spirit, faith, hope—the victory of a noble idea which will and must in the end triumph. . . .

If anyone should see in this record of the outstanding achievements of Jewish resistance and heroism any diminution of the deeds of the Nazi beasts, then that person has not begun to understand the meaning of this song of songs of Jewish spiritual strength.[19]

Gerty Spies expresses a relationship with her writings that verges on solipsism, referring to them as 'creatures' rather that creations. She writes of lying awake at night memorizing her verses: 'I held

18. Ibid., p. 34.
19. Klara Caro, p. 1.

them tight, they held me tight—we held each other. . . .'[20] After the liberation she corresponded with the dramatist Elsa Bernstein, who also survived Theresienstadt, and she quotes Bernstein's views on writing: 'To write a poem means to compromise, to elevate it from the intermediary stage of being and consciousness, to purposely give it form.'[21] The articulation of such overtly literary concepts about the process of composition are rare in writings about Theresienstadt. Grete Salus gives the most simple explanation for having recorded her memories: 'Writing helped me.' She also relates how they came to be published.

> The manuscript remained lying in a drawer. When I emigrated to Israel I took it with me. Years passed. In Israel I happened to meet Count von Spreti, who is now the German Ambassador to Luxemburg: He had visited us several times before the war in Prague. He asked me to tell my story. As we had very little time I remembered the manuscript and gave it to him with the words: 'Here it is. Read it.' Apart from my brother nobody else had ever read it. Thanks to Count von Spreti's mediation many will now be able to read it.[22]

Two of the women refer to the Nobel Prize winner Hermann Hesse's active involvement and interest in their writings. After her release in Switzerland Edith Kramer went to visit Hesse in order to greet him for a mutual friend whom they later learned had perished in Auschwitz. In the following excerpt, which provides additional information about Hesse's feelings towards Nazism, Kramer tells what happened during one of her visits.

> Hermann Hesse asked me to report in detail, even such things as seemed unimportant to me. From his questions I gathered that he never missed anything I had already told him. He encouraged me to write down my experiences and said emphatically that these were quite exceptional and worth recording in all details. He was simply interested in everything. . . .
>
> This was the time (1946) when Hesse was awarded the Nobel-Prize. As his health was not the best, he did not go to Stockholm but a celebration was arranged in Bern instead. He told me that a 'friend' had donated an amount on this occasion. This should be

---

20. *Drei Jahre Theresienstadt*, p. 47.
21. Ibid., p. 4.
22. *Eine Frau Erzählt* , p. 5.

given to a refugee who wanted to continue his or her studies in Switzerland and Hesse recommended me. Thus I received monthly support. I suspect that Hesse himself was the friend, for he did not allow me to thank the anonymous donor. I visited the Hesses also from Zürich several times. One afternoon—we were just sitting at the coffee table—the maid brought a visiting card: Richard Strauss. However, to my regret, Hesse did not receive Strauss. He did not wish to be in contact with people who in his opinion had lacked backbone during Nazi time.[23]

Hesse also corresponded with Spies, who shares a comment made by him about her book of poems: 'It is beautiful. There is something reconciling in the very fact that this Theresienstadt also produced as poetic a book as yours.'[24]

With the exception of Spies and Käthe Starke the difference in the quality of writing between published and unpublished memoirs is not significant. Both Spies and Starke employ a style of writing which distinguishes theirs from the other documents in terms of narrative technique and professional polish. Starke shows considerable skill in her use of irony, while Spies's prose and poetry reveal an appropriately elegiac and lyrical quality. Dormitzer provides the most painstaking documentation of the camp. It is her poetry, however, with its powerful physical imagery that makes the camp come alive. Of all the women Glas-Larsson is probably the most accessible, in that her casual intimate style invites the reader to approach a self-portrait that is often less than flattering. Her memoir is the most honest and revealing and also suggests a development of her character from a naïve girl to a very appealing and courageous older woman. The poet whose work proved to be the most resistant to translation was Gertrud Kantorowicz. A remarkably cerebral poet, her verse makes a mockery of the assertion that Theresienstadt did not produce abstract poetry. One woman in particular commands recognition as a major poet not only of Theresienstadt but of the Holocaust: the poetry of Ilse Blumenthal-Weiss presented not only the greatest challenge to translate but the most profound satisfaction.

My understanding of the word 'survivor' has been challenged and enlarged by the work of Werner Weinberg who finds it constricting and suggestive. He prefers the words 'I alone have escaped to tell you', from the Book of Job.[25] In the aftermath of their experiences

---

23. 'Hell and Rebirth', pp. 27–8. Written in English by Kramer.
24. See 'Tagebuchfragment aus Theresienstadt'.
25. See Weinberg, *Self-Portrait of a Holocaust Survivor*, p. 152.

the predominant sense transmitted through the writings of the women of Theresienstadt is not one of survival in the sense of having lived through and beyond the experience, but of loss and aloneness. But there is also a strong desire to tell, expressed categorically by Glas-Larsson in the words she chose for the title of her memoir, 'Ich will reden' (I want to tell).

The writings selected for this book reflect both the intimacy that has evolved in the course of discovering the subject and the confidence that these writings represent a larger script. Though documents of Theresienstadt may still be discovered, this volume, I believe, offers a fresh perspective of the particular brand of suffering that Theresienstadt fostered and specifically how it affected women and was transmuted by them into lyrical and narrative fragments.

The most rewarding outcome of the collecting together of these fragments would be if Theresienstadt could thereby acquire a new identity, beyond the one imprinted on it by Nazi ideology. That identity can only be won by showing that on the other side of the heavily guarded ramparts there were real people. Many of them were women. Some of these women were rather prim. Some were cultured. One wanted to dye her hair but there was no water. One was ordered to stop crying but refused. One told about how old Mr Falkenstein beat the system. One noted how the Russian horses grazed on the well-kept lawns. One asked to be carried outside to die. She wanted to see the sky. These fragments are, I believe, what the poet and Theresienstadt survivor Ilse Blumenthal-Weiss meant when she wrote:

> Nothing is lost. Everything persists.
> A leaf, a flute song. Meeting again.
> The prison wall; dull dregs.
> The poppy field near harbour town.
>
> The call of love, a hand's firm comfort,
> These all wait, remain, are drawn
> By lot from towns, barns and mirror seas.
> Nothing is lost. Everything wants to belong.[26]

---

26. Quoted in *Mahnmal*, p. 33. The poem is printed in German in Appendix B.

1

The History of Terezin

TEREZIN, or Theresienstadt to give it its Germanized name from November 1941 until 1945, is situated about forty miles north of Prague, near the point where the River Eger flows into the Elbe. Originally built as a garrison town in 1780 by the Emperor Joseph II and named after his mother the Empress Maria Theresa, it was ideally equipped to house about 7000 soldiers and their families. In the course of Theresienstadt's three-and-a-half-year history it housed over 141,000 inmates. Of these around 33,500 died in the camp and 88,000 were transported to extermination centres in Eastern Europe—after October 1942 exclusively to Auschwitz and its satellite camps. Only 3500 survived from these transports. A fort, known as the Little Fortress, was also part of Terezin's structure, though at a little distance from the town itself, and had been used during the First World War as a prison for opponents of the Austro-Hungarian war, when its most famous prisoner was Gavvilo Princip, instigator of the Saravejo assassination. The Gestapo first re-opened the Little Fortress for use as a prison in June 1940, and though it supposedly continued as a place for criminals and political prisoners, it was used as a punishment block for inmates from Theresienstadt, who could be sent to the Little Fortress at the whim of the commandant. Around 30,000 prisoners passed through the Little Fortress, many of them to the extermination camps of the East. Conditions in the Little Fortress were worse than in Theresienstadt itself; many prisoners were kept in solitary confinement and under the threat of execution—a threat that was carried out 2000 times.

The establishment of Theresienstadt as a Jewish ghetto in November 1941 was the culmination of a series of events that had begun with the Nazi occupation of Czechoslovakia in March 1939 and its declaration by the Nazis as a Protectorate. SS General Heydrich came to power in September 1941 and declared martial law. For the Czechoslavic Jews and the 15,000 German Jews who had fled to Czechoslovakia from the Reich, internment was another phase of the escalating harassment to which they had already been subjected, and which had included seizure of property, abolition of all human rights and, after September 1941, the wearing of the yellow Jewish star. Theresienstadt actually seemed to offer a form of hope to the first Jewish Elder Jakob Edelstein, a Czech who had been commissioned by the Nazis to help with the establishment of the ghetto. By October five transports had already left Prague for Poland, and though the destination and purpose of these transports were not clear, the alternative for Jews of remaining in the Protectorate in somewhat familiar surroundings was a lot less threatening. Since immigration by this time was not an option, internment was viewed by Edelstein as a form of rescue—rescue through work.

In its first phase Theresienstadt was supposed to be a collection camp or transit ghetto for Jews from the Protectorate. A work squad of 342 young men, known as the 'Aufbaukommando', was dispatched to the town in November 1941 and given orders to prepare it to receive Jews from the Protectorate. Dr Siegfried Seidl, an SS colonel, was appointed as the first camp commandant. This is how Lederer describes him:

> Seidl was a typical representative of those young Germans who could not bear the memory of Germany's defeat in the First World War. They became ardent Nazis because the Nazi Party promised to avenge this defeat. Though Seidl was but an indifferent organiser, his callous cruelty and his blind submission to orders from his superiors made him an exemplary SS man. Thus, willingly obeying the orders of his superiors, he saw in the Jews mere material to be delivered to the gas-chambers. He had ordered the first executions in the Ghetto. Seidl callously broke all pledges he gave to the 'Yids', since being a German officer he felt under no obligation to such 'vermin'. He amassed riches by taking commissions for supplies reaching Theresienstadt.
>
> He was always immaculately dressed, kept hounds, and spoke in staccato sentences. His eyes were shifty and furtive; he cast sharp, observant glances from aside. His face was narrow, he was tall of stature, and his hair was fair. Seidl never smiled, he could only force himself to a grin. On his desk was a cartoon of a Jew with the inscription: 'Don't get cross, always try a smile'.[1]

The tone that Seidl set for the camp was sustained, with the addition of some grotesque variations, after he left Theresienstadt and was succeeded by two other commandants—Anton Burger and Karl Rahm.

Women are first mentioned on 30 November and 2 December

---

1. *Ghetto Theresienstadt*, p. 74.

1941, when two transports composed of 1000 people each arrived
from Prague and Brno. The new arrivals were billeted under the
most primitive conditions in cold, damp barracks without running
water or heating. Further hardships were introduced on 6 December, when women were transferred to the Dresden barracks and
were forbidden to have contact with men. Penalties for infractions of
this rule were severe. Twenty to forty women shared a room, the
only comfort being that children under twelve could stay with their
mothers, while those over twelve remained with the parent of the
same gender. (Later most children were separated from their parents and housed in separate barracks.)

By the beginning of 1942 it had become clear to the inmates that
Theresienstadt was far from being merely a transit ghetto designed
to provide some form of security, however minimal. They had to
work, and that work was, in fact, brutal drudgery since they had to
virtually re-build a town that had been equipped for a maximum of
7000 people and was now straining to receive thousands each week.
But beyond the overcrowding another factor was emerging which
stamped its imprint on the town and in the end became its trade-
mark. Theresienstadt was turning out to be not a destination but
what Lederer calls 'a genuine floodgate between two different levels
of the same river'.[2] Transports began to leave Theresienstadt in
January 1942 and did not end until the autumn of 1944.

At the end of January 1942 a council of Elders was formed. It had
thirteen members, of whom the most prominent were Edelstein (the
chief Elder), his deputy Otto Zucker, Dr Paul Eppstein from Berlin
and Rabbi Dr Benjamin Murmelstein. Adler describes the group as
'a hostile, divided triumvirate',[3] a view that has been considered too
harsh by another Theresienstadt survivor.[4] Edelstein and Zucker
were both Zionists which possibly accounts for the tensions in the
group. Their power was essentially very limited but their admini-
strative responsibilities, including the invidious task of selecting
people for transports, were enormous. They were responsible for
delegating and supervising duties at various levels of the camp
hierarchy, ranging from Room Elders all the way up to the Central
Buildings' Authority. Hence the inmates had little to do with the
Nazis themselves on a day-to-day basis under normal circumstances.

It is almost impossible to define the social structure of Theresienstadt. Lederer writes:

2. Ibid., p. 22.
3. *Theresienstadt 1941–1945*, p. 115.
4. Ilse Blumenthal-Weiss, 'Das war Theresienstadt'.

The structure of Theresienstadt was different from that of other German concentration camps. There was an ample measure of self-administration, and even a semblance of normal cultural life. . . . Some of its features were reminiscent of ancient slavery, and others of modern totalitarianism, while certain features cannot be clearly defined.[5]

Real power was in the hands of the commandant who was a puppet of headquarters in Berlin. All three commandants epitomized the stereotypical image of Nazi brutality. Burger is described by Lederer as a 'stout, cold-eyed, hatchet-faced'[6] bully who hated the Czechs. The warrant officers who worked under the commandants gained similar reputations for brutality—for example Rudolf Haindl who was hanged for war-crimes in Litomerice in 1948, as were also Seidl and Rahm.

The ethnic composition of the camp changed drastically in the summer of 1942 when thousands of Jews, mostly elderly and often distinguished, arrived from the Reich. Adler provides an excellent summary of the age, condition and background of the newcomers:

> With few exceptions we are talking about old, tired, mostly frail and even dangerously ill people. . . .
>
> They had painted such a rosy picture about the comfortable, cosy conditions in the Old People's Home of the Reich, of Theresienspa, in the health resort Theresienstadt with its charming villas, pensionen and pleasant old people's homes. So they had brought along curtains, vases, family souvenirs and items that were unsuitable for a camp, items of sentimental value, with which they wanted to make their new surroundings more like home. They had packed a few cigarettes and perhaps even a bottle of wine. . . .
>
> Here they were at the station, exhausted and demolished, being yelled at by the SS, by guards and by Jews; the expressions on their faces showed confusion, despair, incredulity, their hand movements were fearful and anxious. . . .
>
> These exhausted people were now supposed to set off on the long trek to the camp without refreshment, laden down with belongings and often unable to go on. Then they were loaded like cattle into lorries or on to the trailer behind a tractor, often so tightly crammed together that they could neither lie down nor sit.

5. *Ghetto Theresienstadt*, pp. 85–6.
6. Ibid., p. 75.

So in order to be driven to the town, they had to stand, ill, over-tired, thirsty, apathetic or screaming, women with their hair undone, invalids on crutches, blind people with trembling limbs. One time a young SS guard, nicknamed SS Children's Home, hurled twenty-seven people off the trailer when he was driving recklessly round a curve. Ten people were killed on the spot, others died in the hospital or were permanently crippled.

The new arrivals sometimes asked at the station or in the 'sluice' if one or two rooms had been reserved for them or expressed the desire to have rooms with a balcony that faced south.[7]

The presence in the camp of groups from various ethnic and social backgrounds contributed to tense living conditions, which were further exacerbated by overcrowding.

By September 1942 58,500 people were living in Theresienstadt and the daily mortality rate was 131; after 17 September deaths were no longer reported in the daily bulletin. In the same month a crematorium with the capacity to dispose of 190 corpses daily was completed and was a source of great pride to the Nazi officials. The presence of prominent people from the military, industry, and especially the arts gave Theresienstadt a distinctly new character, one which the Nazis soon exploited for their own purposes. The most distinguished of these newcomers, called 'Prominenten', were allowed to receive more parcels from home, which often meant the difference between life and death; so many were able to eke out a frugal, if pathetic, existence. These elderly, distinguished people thought that they were coming to a quiet Bohemian town to wait out the turbulent war years in peace. A Czech writer views this as one of the greatest frauds the Nazis perpetrated and adds: 'They end their pilgrimage in a dirty attic or underground cell, where they die within days or weeks, of pneumonia, diarrhoea, of hunger, on the floor, without straw mattresses, without blankets, without medical care.'[8]

A new phase was about to begin which included the promotion of a carefully developed Nazi plan of presenting Theresienstadt as a model ghetto. The first step in the programme was to give the camp the façade of a civilian, peace-time town. To this end streets and blocks lost their numbering system in July 1943 and were given pretty names like 'Riverside'. Barracks were designated for special

7. *Theresienstadt*, p. 107.
8. See *Terezin*, ed. Frantisek Ehrmann, Otta Heitlinger and Rudolf Iltis, p. 27.

purposes, Potemkin stores were opened offering goods confiscated from in-coming transports. Lederer describes them in the following terms:

> Most of the shops were situated near the Magdeburg barracks and any casual visitor would have assumed that everything, even food, could be bought in the Ghetto. On entering the shops he would, however, have discovered that they were stocked from confiscated luggage. While precious objects, valuable food and decent clothing thus 'acquired' were sent to Germany, the shoddiest trash was allocated to the shops for sale. The food shop sold only mustard and a mysterious paste of acrid taste. Yet the real purpose of the shops was to conceal the brutal reality of Theresienstadt. The Germans wanted to foster the belief—for the benefit of any visitor from the outside world— that life in Theresienstadt was normal and that the Jews received fair treatment. Thus some of the loot was sold to the victims. There were cases where some prisoners—after having waited for their turn— bought back their own trousers or shoes.[9]

A post office, bank, petty crimes court, and coffee house were also opened. For aesthetic reasons the death penalty was carried out only in the Little Fortress. The total effect of these efforts to normalize the town gave it what Adler described as 'a ghostlike character'.[10] Essentially nothing had changed; the average work day was ten hours, the normal day's rations were still substitute coffee, a slice of bread, and thin lentil or potato soup for the main meal.

This normalization phase developed into an even more ambitious stage when an embellishment programme was introduced to camp policies, presumably in response to growing awareness in the free world of the existence of death camps. After considerable pressure from the International Red Cross the Nazis had agreed to allow a delegation to inspect the town. Both the Prague Gestapo and Berlin Headquarters appear to have embarked on the beautification programme with enthusiasm, asserting that the people of Theresienstadt would be better off than civilians in the Reich or military personnel. Among other renovations and improvements, all supplied by Jewish labour and expertise, were better plumbing, the establishment of a library of 60,000 books confiscated from Jews, and a school for children with a permanent 'Closed for Holidays'

9. *Ghetto Theresienstadt*, p. 52.
10. *Theresienstadt*, p. 129.

sign. Cultural and religious activities, formerly driven underground, were no longer banned but actively encouraged. Musical instruments, some of which had previously been smuggled in, now appeared in public. The arts flourished without censorship, except among painters, some of whom paid with their lives for having shown Theresienstadt as it really was. The painters Otto Ungar, Bedrich Fritta, Felix Bloch, and Leo Haas were sent to the Little Fortress where Bloch was so cruelly beaten that he died from his injuries.

The arrival from Bialystock on 24 August 1943 of 1260 starving, filthy, bare-footed children introduced to Theresienstadt a word that had chilling implications for future transports eastwards. The children, aged between three and fifteen, refused to go into the shower-rooms and cried: 'No, no! Gas!'[11] After a six-week stay in Theresienstadt, during which they were nursed back to a modest state of health, they left again on 5 October with fifty-three nurses, among them Franz Kafka's sister Ottilie. Their destination was Auschwitz, and there is no further record of them.

In October 1943 a group of Danish Jews arrived in Theresienstadt, and although there were only 456 of them their presence helped to some degree because they had a highly protected status on account of the active role that their king assumed in insisting on their safety.

In November 1943 the camp commandant Anton Burger, who had replaced Seidl the previous June, accused the Jewish Elders of falsifying camp records and ordered a census of the whole camp. This took place on 17 November and of all single events in the camp's history, it has possibly received the most detailed documentation. Burger singled out Edelstein as being responsible for the incorrect statistics and, on the pretext of his having ridden his bicycle beyond camp limits, sent him and his family to Auschwitz in December. In February 1944, however, Burger himself was replaced by a third commandant, Karl Rahm, an Austrian who threw himself wholeheartedly into the beautification of Theresienstadt. Among the orders he issued was: 'The entrance space outside the gate to the mortuary will be bordered with flower beds.'[12] Rahm also ordered the planting of trees outside the urn repository and the erection of a monument in memory of dead Jews.[13] The culmination of the beautification programme came on 23 June when the Red Cross

11. Ibid., p. 208.
12. See *Ghetto Theresienstadt*, p. 111.
13. Ibid., p. 111.

delegation arrived to the sound of the band playing. Verdi's Requiem was performed, and a soccer game was in progress when the guests reached the sportsground.[14] Beyond noting that everything looked new,[15] the visitors apparently did not express any strong reaction to Theresienstadt. They had been given a carefully rehearsed inspection tour, which avoided all buildings that might arouse suspicion. Transport records show that just before the delegates arrived 5000 people were transported, including a group of the mentally ill. In this way the streets looked less crowded. Handicapped people were forbidden to appear in public. Lederer makes the following comment:

> Rahm had done his job brilliantly. He led the inspectors through spotless streets, houses bright in pastel shades, an adorable Maria Theresa village. On cue, a squad of singing Jewish girls, shouldering rakes, marched off to their gardening. White-gloved bakers unloaded fresh bread into a fake store. At another shop, fresh vegetables were displayed—for the first and last time. In the community center, Terezin's orchestra played Mozart. As the inspectors approached a soccer field, a goal was scored according to script.[16]

Rahm's zeal for projecting Theresienstadt as a place of art and pleasure continued even after the visit of the Red Cross. In mid-August 1944 he ordered a film to be made which included a swimming scene along the banks of the River Ohre. Lederer notes that 'the end of the filming was also the end of the embellishment'.[17] Shortly after the film was made, two of its directors—Kurt Gerron and Frantisek Zelenka—were sent to the gas-ovens in Poland. No wonder Adler called the film 'a work of organised insanity'.[18] Käthe Starke used the film title as the title of her memoir, the ironical words 'Der Führer schenkt den Juden eine Stadt'.

High Holidays were duly celebrated in September and the Jewish Elders wished the inmates a happy new year. Adler comments on this: 'It was not even masks any more but masks worn over masks in a distorted mirage.'[19]

An active cultural life persisted till late in 1944. Daring perfor-

14. Ibid., p. 119.
15. Green, *Artist of Terezin*, p. 90.
16. *Ghetto Theresienstadt*, p. 89.
17. Ibid., p. 121.
18. *Theresienstadt*, p. 184.
19. Ibid., p. 157.

mances were put on, many of the Czech ones more daring than the Nazis suspected.

The last six months of the history of Theresienstadt, from October 1944 to May 1945, brought catastrophe as well as liberation. Eppstein was shot in the Little Fortress and Murmelstein was appointed to be Chief Elder. The autumn transports of '44 spared no one, selections became more and more arbitrary, the camp was virtually depleted of male labour (of a population of 11,804 men only 5000 were left) and more and more women assumed their workload. Transports now included members of the Council of Elders. Zucker was sent to Auschwitz in the third October transport and his wife and twelve-year-old son joined him, believing that they were going to another work camp. They too perished. The stretching of racial laws now brought in more people from mixed marriages, so that there was a considerable body of practising Christians in Theresienstadt. In November '44 there were four days of work, mostly for women and children, in the disposing of urns containing the ashes of those who had died in the camp.

Rumours, called 'bonkes', were circulating—mostly spread in the latrines—that the end was near and that liberating armies were on the doorstep. There was open conflict among the SS about whether to reinstate the embellishment programme or to liquidate the camp. The latter appears to have been seriously considered. The only happy event of this period, at least until the liberation, was the departure on 5 February 1945 of 1200 people on a transport to Switzerland. Scepticism about the destination of transports had grown to the point where many refused to join this transport, but the arrival of postcards from Switzerland finally assured the inmates. On 13 April comfortable coaches arrived to transport the Danes home, an event which further cheered all the other inmates and gave new hope for their own release.

A week later Theresienstadt was hit by the most shattering experience of its history, an experience from which it never recovered. Between March and May 1945 some 1500 people arrived on cattle-trucks from the East in such shocking physical condition that the inmates of Theresienstadt looked well-nourished by comparison. Their arrival ended the illusion of Birkenau as a 'family camp'. The first case of typhus was diagnosed among the newcomers on 24 April, and within a short time hundreds had died, including many nurses and doctors who attended the sick and also, ironically, many who had so far survived the rigours of Theresienstadt. Adler describes their condition in the bleakest terms: 'These people no longer had any belief. They believed in nothing and nobody. They did not even believe in themselves. Everything had been extinguished and devalued. There was no such thing for them as a friend, no such thing as a breath of human warmth.'[20]

By 5 May, the camp had been placed under the protection of the International Red Cross; many of the SS guards, including Rahm, had already fled, taking with them ample supplies of food. Murmelstein resigned as Jewish Elder and a new council was formed under the leadership of Baeck. The Russians arrived early on the morning of 9 May and the next day Dunant placed the camp in their hands. During the weeks that followed quarantine, imposed because of the typhus epidemic, was gradually lifted, relatives arrived from every corner of Europe to take their loved-ones home, buses were despatched from the major German and Austrian cities to Theresienstadt, and after long, arduous journeys the inmates of Theresienstadt arrived back in the cities, many now in ruins, that had once been home. A few of them chose to remain, many emigrated to Israel or to the United States. Theresienstadt became again a little garrison town.

20. Ibid., p. 212.

2

Day to Day Life in the Camp

Transportation to Theresienstadt

IT is not surprising that the women who have recorded their experiences of Theresienstadt devote most of their memoirs to the immediate camp experience rather than to events leading up to their deportation or following their release. This is true of Holocaust literature in general.[1] Some of the women, however, preface their memoirs with descriptions of the particular kinds of harassment and intimidation to which they were subjected before being transported to Theresienstadt. There is a recurring pattern in these memoirs— estrangement from neighbours (some of whom were formerly friends), alienation from the immediate community, loss of employment, of personal items, of property, the dreaded letter with an official seal, the knock on the door, usually late at night, and then the journey to the selection depot. Dormitzer's memoir provides a chilling look at the terrors of *Kristallnacht*, in the very city that was later to witness the judgement against those who perpetrated these crimes. On 10 November 1938 Goebbels made the following statement to representatives of the foreign press.

All the rumours that have been circulating about acts of violence against Jews all over the Reich are pure fabrications. Not so much as a hair of their heads has been touched in the whole of Germany, and Jewish property has neither been damaged nor destroyed. If, in fact, there have been minor incidents, it is because the people have been venting their anger about the death of Herr v. Rath.[2]

Dormitzer introduces her memoir of *Kristallnacht* with what she terms a 'matching statement' to that of Goebbels.

It is a known fact that in Nürnberg, Streicher's own city, site of the worst excesses, the SA assembled at 1.30 in the main square,

1. See Marlene Heinemann, *Gender and Destiny*, p. 91.
2. Quoted in Dormitzer, 'Die Kristallnacht', p. 1.

were handed steel bars and battering rams and were also given precise information about the impending devastation and destruction of all Jewish property, as well as directions for the maltreatment of Jews. The actual words of the Nazi leader: 'It is not a matter of a few more or a few less Jews!' It is a fact that Streicher explained in his defence at the Nürnberg Trials that he never incited the people to violent acts against the Jews. A number of Jews were thrown out of windows and down stairs and died, numerous people came seriously wounded to the Jewish hospital in the neighbouring town of Fürth with broken limbs and terrible bruises; there was a large number of suicides.

Scenes at the destruction of Jewish residences: All paintings were cut to pieces. An art collector, owner of a Rembrandt sketch, offered this masterpiece to the invading SA with the words: 'Please do not destroy this unique work, take it with you, it is irreplaceable!' The response was the total destruction of the sketch. A weeping woman implored: 'Couldn't you at least spare the oilpainting of my late husband? 'Leave if you don't want to watch', was the response as the knives were cutting through the picture. And a mother who was holding the picture of her son who had been killed in the First World War had it wrenched out of her hands and stamped on with hob-nailed boots. A SA troop broke into a newly built villa, which was surrounded by beautiful gardens. The woman who owned the villa recognized in the leader of the troop the landscape artist who had designed the gardens at the cost of thousands of marks; when she pointed that out he answered: 'And now I am destroying them again!' The Orthodox Synagogue was burnt to the ground (the Reform one had already been destroyed and torn down in the summer of '38 at Streicher's command), the rubble that covered the street was removed and the bill given to the Jewish community. In Fürth school-age youths had systematically torn down the headstones in the Jewish cemetery; a child had been injured and had to get medical help and the doctor's bill was sent to the Jewish community. Observation of a fireman in Fürth in front of a burning synagogue: 'For twenty-seven years I have been putting out fires; this is the first time that I had to start one!' A well-known Jewish person was supposed to be arrested and because he had gone away on a business trip it was proposed to arrest his wife and his sick child instead. His wife showed them the child lying with a high fever and pointed out that serious harm could be caused if the child were taken away on this cold November night. The answer was: 'All the better, then it will die all the sooner!' It is unnecessary to point out that many children were also taken to the Jewish hospital suffering from head-wounds and the effects of maltreatment. Some sick people who had just been operated on in the hospital had to stand to attention in front of the mobs of SA men as they streamed in and as a result: death by embolism and haemorrhage.

These are just some little excerpts that could be supplemented by hundreds more.'[3]

Elsewhere Dormitzer records the vicious physical assault that the Jews personally experienced on *Kristallnacht*, noting that acts of hostility against Jews were particularly brutal in Nürnberg, where conditions were worse, she claims, than in any other of the major cities, and where Jews were not allowed to go to public parks, swimming pools or restaurants. The SA troops invaded her home twice on *Kristallnacht*. Fifteen SA men came, and on their first visit injured the Dormitzers and destroyed all their furniture and belongings. On the second trip the SA broke into the Dormitzers' bedroom, beat up Else's husband, breaking the bridge of his nose with a steel rod, and finally chased them both into the streets. After a Christian doctor had examined them they left by taxi for the Jewish hospital in Fürth, which had been taken over by the police. Christian nurses had to leave. All the Jewish employees and residents of Fürth were assembled in the town square, the men were sent to Dachau and the women and children were sent home. After spending three days in the hospital they were sent for and taken to a Nazi headquarters called 'House and Garden' where they were forced to relinquish all claim to their property and to sell it. Dormitzer agreed immediately to the sale of her house valued at 150,000 DM for a price of 10,000, which sum was given to the people who would be looking after the house. Later she learned that a cousin who had resisted this forced house sale had been severely beaten.[4]

Two other memoirs focus on the mental and emotional turmoil generated in women through living in constant fear of being evicted from their homes. Though Käthe Breslauer's memoir is framed unambiguously by Nazi Terror, it is threaded with the shadows of people who are kind-hearted, humane and essentially passive. This is how she remembers her deportation, after having received her first notice a year previously:

3. Ibid., pp. 1–2. The SA were the *Sturmabteilung*, the brown-shirted stormtroopers. The SS, refered to frequently elsewhere, were the *Schutzstaffel*, the special security force, also known as the Blackshirts.
4. 'Erlebnisse in Nürnberg', p. 2.

But it was no longer a pleasure, and we felt very isolated; nobody dared to greet us in the street, just sometimes a fearless friend would secretly bring us groceries which were no longer available to us. Some neighbours—the ones who were not Nazis—put milk and other valuables in front of our door. Because the whole neighbourhood knew about our imminent departure we were secretly asked in the street if we had anything to sell: a little table or wardrobe or the like. Whenever the doorbell rang we would be startled, thinking the executioners had come. In the end we were in such a state that we said to each other: it's high time to get out of here, come what may. . . . It is impossible for me to describe how I felt when I left my home. Everything around me seemed unreal. The landlady secretly shaking hands with us, her eyes heavy from sadness, people looking on at the interesting spectacle with gloating smiles . . . the drive from our quiet suburb into the city, where the van periodically stopped to pick up new passengers, crowds staring, some maliciously, others filled with sympathy—everything going by me like a dream—and yet to this day it has remained indelibly printed in my memory.[5]

Eighty-year-old Rosa Salomon was arrested on 6 May, just as she was about to fall asleep. She had prepared herself as best she could, but at a certain point, just as in facing death, no amount of preparation is ever enough.

My son already had his case and a rucksack almost packed but I had virtually nothing ready because I was always un-packing and re-packing for air-raids or for deportation. Despite the fact that I have always been able to meet the most difficult situation with a clear head, this time my nerves completely collapsed when faced with the devastating fact that I was being forcibly dragged out of my bed and out of the home that had already been stripped to the minimum. I left behind all that I had prepared for this eventuality, completely forgetting everything. In addition I was a physical wreck and was not able to carry the luggage that would certainly not have been too much for me under normal conditions. The two stout SS men apparently thought it beneath them to help an old woman with her case. Thus everything literally fell on the shoulders of my son, who was certainly no giant. Because he had to carry my luggage, he made several trips to and from the police station. We stayed all night in the police station. The guards

5. 'Erinnerungen an Theresienstadt', pp. 1–2.

passed the time playing cards.[6]

Hedwig Ems was alone in her apartment when the doorbell rang: 'One morning four or five Gestapo men appeared at the door and, without taking any notice of me, broke the locks to the other rooms, taking everything that appealed to them. I could not see what they had put in their briefcases. . . .'[7] Some time later she received another visit, this time in the evening, from two men from the Gestapo. She continues:

> One of them said: 'I suppose the big-wigs have already taken everything.' The other one told me he was about to get married and was looking for some bedroom furniture with the modern low-slung look. When I told him that my beds were high and old-fashioned (which was true) he said he was not interested and the two of them politely took their leave.[8]

Though anti-semitism existed, Czech Jews were not subjected to the same degree of persecution during the thirties as were Jews in Germany and Austria, which accounts for the re-location of Jews from the Reich in Prague after 1933. The memoir of Margareta Glas-Larsson, one of the most anecdotal in style and content, reveals a degree of assimilation that is nothing short of the repudiation of Jewishness. It also betrays perceptions of women and specifically of Jewish women that are demeaning and degrading. This is how she describes her husband and, unwittingly, his repudiation of his Jewishness:

> He was twenty-one. He was very arrogant, a baptized Jew, Shorschi Glas, very Catholic, with a great aversion towards certain types of Jewish faces. He had been spoiled rotten and had been badly brought up. . . . He got five schillings—at that time a lot of money—when he didn't come home for dinner. . . . And before we met he had spent a year in Paris to learn banking. The bank manager wrote to my father-in-law saying that he saw him three times. . . . I fell madly in love with him but was for him only a little girl whom he barely noticed. But he was my idol and the only thing I wanted in life was to marry him. I was only sixteen.[9]

6. 'Erlebnisse einer Achtzigjährigen im KZ Theresienstadt', p. 2.
7. Hedwig Ems, p. 4.
8. Ibid.
9. *Ich will Reden*, p. 78.

A year later he did indeed marry her. Her narrative continues with this description of their marriage: 'My marriage was not an easy one. He still had a girlfriend who really loved him, a very blonde Sudeten German. He said, "You know, I basically only love blonde women." And so I said: "And yet you married one with black hair. That's the way it always is." '[10]

Arrival and First Impressions

First impressions of Theresienstadt are mong the bleakest in Holocaust literature, not because it was the worst concentration camp but because it bore no resemblance to the descriptions that people had been given of it before they arrived. Some people were even known to have given bribes to the SS to gain admission to this spa Theresienbad. Shock and disappointment were clearly contributing factors in the deaths of many people, particularly the elderly, after their arrival. Dormitzer, for example, was advised by the SS in Amsterdam to take along sensible shoes for country walks. Others write about packing satin dresses for evening attire. Dormitzer continues:

> After a journey of at least thirty hours we arrived in Bauschowitz and had to walk with our luggage to Theresienstadt, where our money was taken from us and also anything else that appealed to those in charge. I was happy to be able to rescue my medicine bag. The 'strip and search' room for our transport was in the Aussiger Barracks. It would be pointless to add that all the favours they had promised in Amsterdam turned out to be lies. Upon our arrival in Theresienstadt my husband and I suffered the typical admission shock which paralysed one's whole being. My husband was never able to recover, but on the second day I pulled myself together, recognizing that there was no other way to survive in the place. . . . My husband and I were separated immediately but at least lodged in the same house, with seventeen to a small room. Both of us—like all the other inmates—lying on the floor on a little hard straw mattress, neither table nor chair, neither nail in the wall nor wardrobe nor drawers. Food was served after queuing for a long time in all kinds of weather in the courtyards. In addition we were forbidden to go outside or to turn on the lights (the whole town was generally punished if one individual disobeyed), which meant that we had to spend some

10. Ibid.

weeks in the desolate courtyard and when darkness fell had to sit in the dark. All household chores were done by us—cleaning, sweeping, washing—and besides this every inmate, whether old or young, had to do general work duty. At the beginning it was an eight-hour day, later a ten-hour day. There were no days off, not even for High Holidays. We were often unable to recognize people from our native city who came to visit us—emaciated skeletons with dull, fixed stares, broken people. Many whom we enquired about, among them our closest relatives (brother, brother-in-law, sister-in-law, cousins) were already dead, some by suicide.[11]

The Dormitzers had once enjoyed prestige and prosperity with the kinds of freedom and privilege that this lifestyle implies. Now they were not only deprived of mutual support and comfort but were thrown into squalid living conditions. Original works of art were replaced by bare, damp walls, without even a nail to hang clothes on. Added to this was the oppressive sense of guilt and accountability that weighed on all. One infraction of camp rules brought punishment on all. From an official camp record one of the consequences noted by the Nazis of a ruptured family life was the effect on women, 'apathy, neglect, hysterical outbursts'.[12]

Käthe Breslauer's pre-conception of Theresienstadt, shaped in Berlin largely by rumour, though not so specific as Dormitzer's, was still a positive one. 'The rumour was going round Berlin that Theresienstadt consisted of good hospitals and old people's homes. Even if we didn't believe everything, we hoped that it would be at least tolerable.'[13] These rumours were, however, dispelled before the Breslauer sisters even reached the gates of Theresienstadt.

On the way our helpers told us about all the suffering that awaited us in Theresienstadt: poor living conditions, hunger and the absence of minimal comforts, the very opposite from what we had been told in Berlin. During my very first days I saw in the streets one of the most unpleasant sights of my whole stay in Theresienstadt: unending long lines of old, broken people were shuffling along in the direction of the Bauschowitz railway station—a transport to the East! It is a good thing we did not know till the end of the war what these transports meant, but we did suspect that they did not mean anything good and were a change for the

11. 'Erlebnisse in Nürnberg', p. 3.
12. See Adler, *Theresienstadt 1941–1945*, p. 415.
13. 'Erinnerungen an Theresienstadt', p. 1.

worse over Theresienstadt.[14]

No attempt was made on the part of fellow-sufferers to delude them further. It is, however, equally striking that no attempt was made to comfort them, in view of the appalling conditions that awaited them.

Adler perceives the attitude of German Jews to their new situation as stemming from a certain ignorance, which he attributes to the degree of assimilation they had previously experienced in the mainstream of German life.

> The average German Jew did not comprehend what the camp was all about. They had been helplessly thrown into a situation which they did not understand. An advanced stage of assimilation took bitter revenge on them. . . .
>
> The majority of German Jews were from liberal circles, such as those from the 'Central Union of German-Jewish Citizens'. With one blow the foundation of their bourgeois lifestyle had been removed and many were too old or helpless to be able emotionally to replace this loss, and because not all of them were impoverished immediately the collapse of their world scarcely hit home to them. A few of them were completely alienated from Judaism and, unshaken by events, felt German. Those who had any sense kept quiet about it. Some, however, who had been baptized and other half-Jews who passed themselves off in a tragi-comical way as Germans in these surroundings and did not want to hear about Jews or even Czech Jews, even maintained that 'the Jews are to blame for everything that is happening here', or 'if the Führer were to know what's going on, then everything would be different; he simply doesn't know or he would never put up with it'.[15]

First impressions recorded in two of the memoirs contain visual reminders of death that destroy any illusion of Theresienstadt as a benign place and underscore its macabre and ghastly character. Here is Clara Eisenkraft:

> First impression on our arrival: a hearse. But no horses. People were pulling it. And there were no coffins. Bread was being transported in it. A whole hearse filled with loaves of bread for exiled people. Later we got used to the sight. After our hand-luggage had been pilfered we were led through the place. Incredi-

14. Ibid., p. 2.
15. *Theresienstadt*, pp. 304–5.

ble! Where were the old people's home and the living quarters we had been told about? Where were the clean houses where each person was to have his own well-furnished room? Through the open doors we could see figures in rags lying on the floor or on wooden frames. Groups of miserable-looking people were being led to get their food; each carried a little bowl.[16]

The degradation of people into animals is another aspect of the concentration camp experience. In Theresienstadt, however, there is another side to this degradation. Leo Baeck, who also had to pull a cart, said later at the Hebrew Union College that they used to talk about Plato while doing so. Perhaps Baeck was one of the intellectuals Breslauer noticed. She writes: 'One could see in the streets elderly distinguished-looking gentlemen whom one could recognize as intellectuals, sweeping the streets and doing similar work.'[17] On a less philosophical note, some youths were said to have sung Chopin's Funeral March while pulling the cart.

Alexandra Sternberg's first glimpse of the camp is no less disheartening: 'Our first sight upon arriving in Theresienstadt was of young men who had been hanged on trees, for having attempted to post letters illegally.'[18] This was in fact not an uncommon sight, especially in the earlier days of the camp when people were also hanged for being caught smoking cigarettes.

Another view of Theresienstadt, grotesque and ironic, is offered by Glas-Larsson. She had been interned for months under deplorable conditions in Prague and was being sent to the notorious Little Fortress, but at this point did not realize the full implications of her situation. She relates the following incident regarding her arrival:

A really young SS man sitting beside me said, 'You have come to a real paradise but just wait till you get to Auschwitz-Birkenau. They'll shave off your hair there. You'll only be a number. You'll get two months and then into the gas-chamber.' He looked at me, and then took another look. 'You don't even look like a Jew. You don't have a Jewish nose. Actually it's a pity about you.'

Then I saw a man wrapped in rags with a Yellow Star, absolutely pale, on crutches. And I looked and said, 'No, that's not my husband; it can't be my husband, it is not. . . .' Then we were marched one by one into the guard room. 'Glas, come in!'

16. *Damals in Theresienstadt*, p. 35.
17. 'Erinnerungen an Theresienstadt', p. 4.
18. Alexandra Sternberg, p. 2.

There was a commandant who said, 'Your name is Glas? We have another Glas here. Is that your husband?'

So it was my husband whom I had not recognized.[19]

Glas-Larsson was thus affronted on three fundamental levels— that of her Jewishness, that she would not survive, and that even if she did she would become like the person whom she barely recognized as her husband. The fact that she recalls this incident so vividly as a woman in her seventies shown how strongly the SS man's message had become embedded in her consciousness. The anecdote also links retrospectively with the description (see above p. 25) of her 'very Catholic' husband and underscores the terrible irony of his rags and yellow star.

Salomon describes her anxiety when she was separated from her son: 'I did not know where my son was. To my great consternation men and women were immediately separated upon arrival. I later found out that he had been lodged in the Hannover Barracks. But initially I was in a terrible state about him and sick with worry I ventured out of the sleeping quarters.'[20] In the courtyard outside she saw a water tap and writes: 'I later learned that we were not allowed to wash here but only use it for drinking water and for washing dishes. This entailed queuing for a long time'.[21] Her narrative continues with a description of her first experience of the Theresienstadt latrines. 'When I went along the dark, rough corridor for the first time, saw the five holes side by side and smelled the stink of chlorine and lysol, I almost passed out. In the end my only option was to use these facilities that were an insult to decency, along with everybody else, high and low, and in fact to queue when they were most in use, in the morning and evening.'[22] She points out that many of the women who cleaned the latrines were from high ranks of society, and kept cross-infection in check by their vigour. This attitude reveals remarkable fortitude and resilience and proves that these qualities can defy age barriers under the most abominable conditions. It is also interesting to note that the threat of disease demolished class distinctions and united women from different echelons of society in a joint fight against it.

Käthe Starke's first view of Theresienstadt was from the barrack window: 'It was crawling with people below. Opposite, the Magdeburger Barrack's gates sucked in a stream of people and spat them

---

19. *Ich will Reden*, p. 115.
20. 'Erlebnisse einer Achtzigjährigen', p. 4.
21. Ibid.
22. Ibid., p. 5.

out again, a strange lifeless mass enveloped in a cloud of dust that had been raised by their tired, shuffling feet. They were all carrying receptacles, some of them appeared to be full. And all were wearing the yellow star.'[23] A similar scene is captured by Malvina Schalkova (plate 1). She also narrates that upon arrival some people magnanimously offered bread and sugar to former acquaintances whom they had recognized but their gallant gesture was turned down with the words: 'Don't ever give away anything edible here!'[24]

Marlene Heinemann discerns a noticeable spirit of selfishness in Holocaust writing. 'One of the curiosities of Holocaust memoirs is that the vast majority contain contradictory evidence about the predominance of selfishness over cooperation in the concentration and death camps. General statements about helping and comradeship stand side by side with assertions that the Nazi system set people against each other and that selfish responses were the norm.'[25] Many of the Theresienstadt memoirs bear this out. The crowded conditions produced irritability, nervousness and downright hostility, especially at night when everybody craved sleep. A particular kind of torture in Theresienstadt was the repeated transfer of people to different rooms and barracks, presumably to deter friendships and discourage solidarity among the inmates. Eisenkraft recalls one of her moves and its effects on others:

Once more I had to sleep on the floor in a rather small, narrow room with sixteen people in two rows. Because the room was also very narrow we were not able to stretch our legs or we would bump into those lying opposite. Apart from this we had to keep a passage clear for those who had to go out during the night. I was not given much of a welcome for the room was already overcrowded. My neighbours to the right and left of me complained bitterly when they had to make room for me between them. . . . Every morning there was a lot of bickering when beds were being made. 'You pushed your mattress on to my area,' was the general complaint. 'These five centimetres belong to me.' This is how they argued back and forth, making life into a real hell. And whenever I stretched my legs out in my sleep, I would be pushed back with a rough kick and of course would wake up and not be able to go back to sleep again. That's when I cried. And like the prodigal son I used to think of my good home and our happy family life, and

---

23. *Der Führer schenkt den Juden eine Stadt*, p. 34.
24. Ibid.
25. *Gender and Destiny*, p. 81.

like him I would have gladly chosen to be the lowest worker in our factory, to live as well and be able to sleep.[26]

It is interesting to find a New Testament allusion in this narrative, in which Eisenkraft explicitly compares herself to the son who had wilfully strayed and left the Father's house and found himself in animal-like conditions while the very servants at home were eating better than he.

Dormitzer also relates experiences with frequent moving, but she focuses on the physical hardships rather than the effects on human relationships:

> The constant moving from one room to another, from one house and one barracks to another, mostly within the space of an hour or less, was accompanied by numerous yellings and at great personal cost (we had to give the men who helped us move our luggage bread or other groceries). I myself moved seventeen times. In the summer of '43, for example, the Sudeten barracks in which 5000 men were living had to be cleared within forty-eight hours and its inmates were crammed into already overcrowded barracks. The beds were so close to one another that it was impossible to keep a passageway clear between them, which was, of course, extremely unhygienic.[27]

A Czech psychologist provides a concise summary of these hardships: 'Chronic frustration increased the significance of completely secondary things in ordinary life. There was an increase in quarrels over trifles: for a better bed, a larger piece of bread, the slightest possibility of distinguishing oneself.'[28]

But even in such depressing and unpleasant conditions there was such a thing as camp routine and even cause for a minor if muted celebration, as the memoir of Paula Frahm, a blind woman, testifies. (Thirty blind people had been transported to Theresienstadt in August 1942 and seventy deaf-mutes in September 1942.)

> Somehow or other life settled down. We got up at 6.00 a.m. We took turns to wash for our aides had been able to procure three wash basins for eighteen people. Then we had coffee, an undefinable drink, that was usually not even warm. . . . The distribution of five pieces of lavatory paper per person was a time of jubilation;

---

26. *Damals in Theresienstadt*, p. 33.
27. 'Leben in Theresienstadt', p. 3.
28. See *Terezin*, ed. Frantisek Ehrmann, Otta Heitlinger and Rudolf Iltis, p. 135.

the little piece of soap we received now and then was guarded like the greatest luxury and in this way we stolidly faced the day.[29]

The following excerpts from Dormitzer's memoirs provide further miscellaneous facts that add to a more complete understanding of daily life in Theresienstadt:

Officially we were allowed to write a thirty-word postcard every month, later every two months, and depending on the mood of the CO incoming or outgoing mail was thrown into the fire.

I should also mention the so-called money and cigarette controls, during which people had to leave their rooms; everything was carefully examined by four people who took with them anything that appealed to them. Theresienstadt had its own currency, on which was printed Moses with the tablets of the Law. Part of our wages was paid with this and periodically we could make small purchases, for example, mustard, celery salt, substitute tea but never bread or proper nourishment, also underwear and clothes—all stolen from suitcases. Luggage was never delivered to Jews who had been deported from Germany. It is understandable that this kind of life brought out every bad human characteristic; theft of all kinds, mostly food items, was the order of the day. Children were trained to steal and parents of those who were skilled in stealing potatoes were envied. . . . Certain offences, such as the possession of tobacco or money (both strictly forbidden), resulted in removal to the Little Fortress, which was under the control of the Germans, and meant for the most part that the person did not come back. Along with physical maltreatment was also the perpetual state of turmoil in which we were kept. All commands and orders came at night, sometimes the light had to be kept on for an hour and no reason was given. Visits from Control Commissions were announced beforehand which meant a downright unbearable workload for the houses—(cleaning, clearing up, sweeping). The commission hardly ever came. Air-raid alerts at the oddest times, without a plane in sight, kept us standing for hours in strange hallways, mostly at mealtimes.[30]

Ethnic Groups

Another shock for new-comers was the strained relationships be-

29. 'Theresienstadt von einer Blinden erlebt und niedergeschrieben', p. 3.
30. Dormitzer, 'Leben in Theresienstadt', pp. 4–5.

tween Jews from Germany, Czechoslovakia and Austria. Relationships between Austrian and Czech Jews, though not always amicable, do not appear to have been so fragile as those between Austrian and German Jews. The worst tensions occurred between Czech and German Jews. Adler gives a detailed account of the various groups conceding, somewhat grudgingly one feels, the quality of uprightness to the German Jews. The overall impression he gives, however, is that they were dull in their understanding.

German and Austrian Jews were unified only by their common language. The Austrians were almost exclusively from Vienna and their character at times revealed a faint glimmer of their Eastern origin. The German Jews were regionally varied in speech pattern and character traits—Saxons, Rhinelanders, Franks, Swabians, Bavarians, Berliners, Hamburgers and Schlesiens could, with practice, be recognized. It was their practical attitude to everyday affairs that separated the Viennese, in this regard like the Czech Jews, from the German Jews. Their common plight, on the other hand, united these two groups but separated them from the Czechs.

The average German Jew did not comprehend what the camp was all about. They had been helplessly thrown into a situation which they did not understand. An advanced stage of assimilation took bitter revenge on them. They were so used to giving obedience and blind confidence to an authoritarian state that they had to feel Hitler's whip on their own bodies to make them take notice. Even then their conclusion was often clouded and ascribed blame for camp conditions to misunderstandings rather than to the SS or simply to internal management. The Germany of 1942 often seemed to these people to be that of 1900. They were often obstinate, pedantic and in respect to their circumstances, particularly in details, tragi-comically correct. They kept a greater distance than did other groups from Jewish matters apart from religious traditions. Only a few were Zionists. A significant number were only Jewish in the sense of the 'racial laws' and that does not include the many who had been christened and the ones from mixed marriages. Germans from the Reich were handicapped by their difficulty in understanding camp jargon with its mixture of old Austrian military language and sprinklings of Czech, Slavisms, Nazi-German and Zionist expressions, Theresienstadt coined words, and Bohemian-Moravian dialect. In this respect the Viennese had an easier time. The prim and proper manner of many German Jews made them often appear to others as dense.

They were not crafty and were not so able to see through things as were the Czech Jews who were, in fact, less upright but far more clever and humorous. . . .[31]

The memoir of the eighty-year-old Berlin woman Rosa Salomon provides a mild correction to this dull image, even if the humour is unintended.

> The Czechs are a very different breed of people. The women have a proud bearing and are enormous, regular valkyrie. I have never seen such large people, not even in Sweden, Siegfried and Günther types. One would have anticipated a certain bonding and solidarity, since they too had been robbed of home, possessions and an existence, had been separated from loved ones just as forcibly as we, had also to live in a concentration camp. But nothing of the sort happened. For them we were not persecuted fellow-believers but hated Germans. . . . A relative of mine was introduced to another person as 'a nice person, even though she is a German'. Our Czech brothers were superior to us in that they could speak German and Czech. They could understand us but we could not understand them, for they always spoke Czech and addressed us in German only when they absolutely wanted to or had to. They were superior to us in every way, had Prague and friends nearby, so that they were well provided for with packages and good things and did not suffer the same degree of undernourishment and weight loss as we did.[32]

Starke contends that she was treated more like a German than a Jew in Theresienstadt and adds: 'Something my father used to say proved to be true. Initially when emigration was discussed he had expressed the opinion that he saw no sense in it, for although they were indeed Jews in Germany, abroad they would be Germans. In Theresienstadt we were Germans.'[33] She also narrates an anecdote about an encounter between a Czech couple from the élite work squad and a German newcomer. The story strongly suggests that the incident was handled by the German woman, and in fact by Starke herself, with aplomb and humour.

> Even in the first days we had to correct some naïve and false

31. Adler, *Theresienstadt*, p. 304.
32. 'Erlebnisse einer Achtzigjährigen', p. 6.
33. *Der Führer schenkt den Juden eine Stadt*, p. 56.

misconceptions. We thought that we were Jews coming to Jews and that everybody would be equal. But nothing of the sort. Irma Zancker was the first to be taught a lesson. To her great delight she had discovered one morning, shortly after our arrival, her lovely clean luxurious mattress in the courtyard of our building. The label with her name was still sewn on it. A young couple, busy making a wooden frame for it, turned to her indignantly when she approached them. 'Hello,' she said in a friendly greeting, 'that's my mattress.' And glancing at the wood, she asked, 'Where can you pick this up?' She did not get any answer. The young people resumed their work and expressed their outrage by turning their backs on her.[34]

Edith Kramer gives another anecdote providing a glimmer of humour in this rather bleak landscape of tense relationships:

One should not imagine that living together in such a mass quarter was harmonious. The hopeless situation made people desperate, even aggressive. A great deal of diplomacy was needed to quieten down the exasperated inmates. Nevertheless, even in this hopeless situation there were occasional humorous moments. I remember once when on top of all the noise a young girl was singing 'In diesen heil'gen Hallen kennt man die Rache nicht'.[35]

Ems's memoir contains the strongest language of all the women. She writes: 'The Czechs hated us just as much as we hated Hitler and they held us responsible for the calamity that had hit them. They did not see us as fellow-sufferers but only as Germans, whom they hated.'[36]

Gertrude Schneider, a survivor of the Riga Ghetto, Kaiserwald and Stutthof experienced similar tensions in the course of her numerous internments and made the following statement at a conference on the Holocaust:

I was lucky. Most of the time I was with my mother and my sister. However, I did have friends among the other Viennese girls and the girls from Prague who had come from Theresienstadt with the earliest transport. Somehow the Viennese and Czech Jews kept together more than the German Jews. The German Jews looked

34. Ibid., p. 55.
35. 'Within these hallowed walls revenge is unknown', a well-known aria from *The Magic Flute*. Kramer, 'As a doctor in Theresienstadt', p. 5.
36. Hedwig Ems, p. 6.

down on us. You see, there are hierarchies among Jews and people don't often address themselves to the subject. The Viennese looked down on the Ostjuden and the German Jews looked down on the Viennese Jews and so you stayed with your own in order to avoid conflict.[37]

An exception to the stereotypical pattern that has invaded most of the memoirs offers one of the more gentle and sad touches in the delicate issue of ethnic compatibility. Kramer tells the story:

My room mates were well able to speak German but talked to each other in Czech. I felt their hostility towards me who spoke Hitler's language. They held me responsible for the Nazis. Fortunately there was one exception. A colleague from Prague, Dr Anna Krasa, offered to share her bed with me. She was the only one who was friendly towards me. We had many interests in common. She was very musical, a good pianist. I still remember to what lengths she went to get the use of a piano for practising. There were only a few instruments in the camp so Anna had to play early in the morning, say from 5.00–6.00 a.m. The previous evening she would take the music to bed and hum the tunes to herself. Unfortunately Anna was deported to the East in 1944 and I never saw her again.[38]

Occasionally there are references to kind treatment at the hands of non-Jews, one in very positive terms. Sternberg writes about a Czech SS man named Styassry who stole tomatoes for the women and encouraged them to keep going, for the Russians would soon be coming to liberate them. She writes: 'Among the Czech SS there were many who had been forced into this service and loathed it. If there had not been a group of decent men among them, no Jew would ever have survived.'[39] Frahm confirms this when she points out that the blind were well treated by the Czech women who often gave them food.[40]

Dormitzer's memories of occasional encounters with German SS men are scrupulously compared with the brutal treatment in other camps but still emerge as painful:

37. Quoted in *Women Surviving the Holocaust*, ed. Esther Katz and Joan Miriam Ringelheim, p. 145.
38. 'As a doctor in Theresienstadt', p. 6.
39. Alexandra Sternberg, p. 3.
40. 'Theresienstadt von einer Blinden erlebt', p. 4.

Our treatment on the part of the Germans cannot be compared with that of Auschwitz, Buchenwald or similar concentration camps. In our daily routine we inmates had nothing to do with the Germans but were kept separately and were under Jewish supervision at work (Jewish Regulations Service, ghetto tribunal for thefts, disobedience etc., Labour court, house and room-elders for cleanliness, order and discipline in the houses). During the occasional encounters with Germans there were, of course, slaps on the ear, beatings with sticks and maltreatment, especially when transports were leaving and people did not get into the train fast enough.[41]

Food and the Lack of It

Food, memories of it, missing it, craving it, dreaming of it, in short, the obsession with food colours all the Theresienstadt memoirs. Schneider had this to say, when asked what women talked about during internment: 'You know, the main topic of conversation was food, the most beautiful recipes that anybody could think of, and also a hot bath as soon as the war was over.'[42] Cernyak-Spatz, a survivor of Theresienstadt, added: 'The funny thing was that many of us were of an age group that had never been to cookery classes, but we had the wildest imagination about what we would cook. I don't think I ever became so good a cook as I was with my mouth.'[43]

The following poem by Else Dormitzer captures the terrible anguish of starving people waiting in vain for second helpings of soup, known as 'Nachshub' (reinforcements).

Reinforcements

Snow and ice, wet tempest and hail,
On the skittery streets gaunt figures group
Holding a tin mug in their hands;
Openly or furtively they look for seconds
To bring back to the barrack-wail.
They shuffle along with their cans,
Each from horror and fear pale:
Will there be a little soup?
We really need it just to have breath,
Can we get it without dockets?

41. 'Leben in Theresienstadt', p. 3.
42. Quoted in *Women Surviving the Holocaust*, ed. Katz and Ringelheim, p. 153.
43. Ibid.

In every case they holler, 'wait, wait';
They wait in hollow sockets
Of silence, slowly the seconds sweat.
Warm your hands, stretch your limbs
Stamp up and down without a feed.
Between stomach noises you hear men roar like rockets,
Beastly ones who, to satisfy their dope-
Like rush for power, need
To be cruel to those who wait and wait.
It's two on the clock—it's not too late
To see or smell the steaming pot.
Then an order crows in the distance:
'Today there are no reinforcements.'
The beast on duty drives off the lot,
They turn away without resistance
Back to their cells
And when next day comes they beg again for portions
On their way to the place of skulls.[44]

Charlotte Buřsova evokes the same despair visually (plate 6), and Inge Auerbacher, who spent three years in Theresienstadt between the ages of seven and ten, gives the following bleak description of meal-times:

Most of the kitchens were located in the open courtyards of the huge barracks. The lines were always very long. It was especially hard in the winter, waiting in the bitter cold. Breakfast consisted of coffee, a muddy-looking liquid, which always had a horrible taste. Lunch was a watery soup, a potato, and a small portion of turnips or so-called meat sauce; and dinner was soup. By the time the people reached the barrels from which the food was ladled out, they were so hungry and exhausted that they immediately gulped their portion down.[45]

She also captured this painful childhood memory in verse.[46] It is clear that the food was poor not because of the preparation but because of the ingredients. Elsa Oestreicher was a gourmet cook, who had managed her own cookery school in Berlin and was now in charge of one of the kitchens in Theresienstadt, attempting to make

44. *Theresienstädter Bilder*, pp. 9–10. The poem is printed in German in Appendix A.
45. *I am a Star*, p. 47.
46. This poem, 'Soup', is reproduced in *I am a Star*.

soup with lentils as the sole ingredient. Malvina Schalkova portrays the grimness of work in the kitchens (plate 4), and Dormitzer describes the typical day's fare as substitute coffee for breakfast, for lunch soup made from potatoes, many of them rotten, a tablespoon of sauce or stew, with the occasional piece of meat, again often rotten; this was alternated with lentil soup and a little flour dumpling. Portions of bread were supposed to last three days. Additionally, there was a weekly ration of 60 gr. of margarine, jam or a strong-tasting sandwich spread.[47] Breslauer has this to say about hunger:

> In earlier years when I read that in famine-affected areas people looked for food in garbage dumps I could not believe such a thing was possible. Here I not only saw that it was possible but that it was a bald fact. Vegetable remains, potato peelings were treasures.[48]

And Zdenka Morsel writes:

> Food was lacking in nourishment and scarce. If once in a blue moon we were given meat scraps, it was horse flesh, and there was more bad smell from it in the room than meat in the gravy. Most meals were simply soups made of powder, with lonely potatoes or lentils swimming in them. Bread was rationed—one slice a day. Once a month or so we were given margarine and a little sugar.[49]

The temptation to encroach upon the following day's bread ration was always great, as Auerbacher recalls: 'I remember Mama marking off each day on our rationed loaf of bread to make certain that we would have enough left to last us a week. This was often difficult. When the hunger pains became too strong, she regretfully cut slightly into the next day's portion of bread.'[50] Another of her childhood memories adds a whimsical note to the landscape of hunger: 'I made a bed for my doll in a cardboard box at the head of my upper-level bunk bed. One day I discovered a dead mouse in it, another victim of starvation. Not even a mouse could find enough leftover crumbs of bread to survive.'[51]

The ritual of bread delivery and distribution elicits the response of

47. 'Leben in Theresienstadt', p. 2.
48. 'Erinnerungen an Theresienstadt', p. 9.
49. Quoted in *Women in the Resistance and in the Holocaust*, ed. Vera Laska, p. 236.
50. *I am a Star*, p. 48.
51. Ibid., p.51.

revulsion in several memoirs. Hedwig Ems writes of the women delivering bread: 'They were holding the bread in their hands which were filthy or with their greasy gloves or pressing it against their stained coats. It was revolting. . . .'[52] A Czech writer also comments on the transport of bread.

> The only means of transportation in the town were worn-out hearses that had belonged to the former religious communities and had been gathered here. Old people, living and dead, were carried in the hearses, but also bread, horse meat, potatoes—everything—went into these once pompous, now decrepit, carriages, pulled by men hitched to them as draft animals.'[53]

An excerpt from the diary of Helga Weissova expresses the exasperation of a fifteen-year-old: 'Everything is transported in hearses here: dirty linen, bread . . . what's the difference, one cart is like another, and so far no one seems to wonder at it, but to transport people in them, that's a little too much.'[54]

The records show that in general women coped with hunger and malnutrition better than men.

> One of the interesting gender-specific distinctions between men and women in the camps was the different reaction to hunger and malnutrition. In medical reports from the Warsaw Ghetto during 1941, in Gurs and in Theresienstadt, 1941–43, memoirs and other administrative reports on women prisoners reveal that women tolerated hunger better than men and survived starvation for longer periods than male inmates. Apparently, women had better strategies for sharing and extending the limited supplies of food; in the pre-war years, women had served as cooks, preparing the family meals and as a result learned ways of extending food in times of need. Previous patterns of behavior, housekeeping skills and habits clearly affected and improved women's chances of survival.[55]

The habit of thinking of the needs of others first did not readily leave women. They grieved to see their men weakened and debilitated, and frequently expressed the opinion that though *they* might possibly survive on the meagre rations the men never would.

---

52. Hedwig Ems, p. 14.
53. Quoted in *Terezin*, ed. Ehrmann, Heitlinger and Iltis, p. 209.
54. Quoted ibid., p. 107.
55. Quoted in *Women Surviving the Holocaust*, ed. Katz and Ringelheim, p. 17.

The difference for many between starvation and a modest level of survival was the food parcel from home. Parcels were in fact more than a life-line to nutrition and could be a measure of a person's worth, revealing vital aspects of an inmate's relationships in the home country, both to immediate family and to non-Jewish friends. In the case of the 439 Danish Jews they reflected the personal concern of the Danish king who sent parcels regularly to the Danish Jews, considered the most privileged of all the groups. The Prague Jews also enjoyed a certain degree of privilege because of their proximity to their home city and in many cases to caring friends. The Dutch were considered the least endowed with food parcels.

Queuing for food one day, Eisenkraft got into conversation with a woman from Vienna who said that she had been interned for two years. When Eisenkraft asked her how she had been able to survive the woman replied: 'I didn't think I would at the first. But ever since my Aryan friends from Vienna have been sending me packages I can make it.'[56] Eisenkraft adds that this was particularly true for inmates from Vienna.

Food parcels not only provided much-needed protein and vitamins but assured inmates that their loved-ones were still alive. Eisenkraft remembers her first parcel: 'I still remember how I felt when after six weeks my first package arrived and I recognized my son's handwriting. It was like a piece of heaven on earth for me. And then the next week a package came addressed in my daughter's writing.'[57]

Not all were so fortunate as Eisenkraft, who received parcels during her entire internment. Spies relates the experience of a woman named Flora Heidingsfelder, nicknamed Heidi, who received only one parcel during her internment. Her response defies the camp stereotype of selfishness discussed earlier. As a result of chronic malnourishment she had developed heart trouble. Spies describes the day her parcel arrived:

It was a big day for Heidi. She asked me to accompany her to the post office. She was really happy and could not believe that she now was one of the fortunate people getting a parcel. Sardines, dates and figs from Portugal! Her face was shining and we hurried back to the barrack, where I discreetly allowed her to enjoy her treasure undisturbed. But what happened? 'Heidi' opened it, took out the contents and beaming with joy proceeded

56. *Damals in Theresienstadt*, p. 27.
57. Ibid.

to share her only parcel with the twenty-five women in the room.[58]

Heidi was later transported, and died in Auschwitz.

Starke relates with pathos and irony an incident involving the widow of a prominent High Court Councillor. Because of her previous social standing this woman lived in the barrack for prominent people.

> Hofrätin Beck was also expecting a little parcel from home, optimistic and composed. Her nephew, who had been like a son to her, would certainly remember her.
>
> She had been in the camp since April 1943 and still had lots of courage left. She did not look her seventy-four years. Her warm cheerfulness, her helpfulness were a blessing to those around her. When notices were distributed about packages, she waited patiently for one but none came. She got thinner and thinner, more and more quiet and finally was too weak to get up. Then a package came in the winter of '44–45. I don't know from whom nor if she even cared; but I do know that she was not able to take even one spoonful of the pudding they made from the dried milk the parcel contained. She was in the advanced stage of intestinal disease.[59]

Health and Disease

Coping with every kind of vermin appears to have demanded enormous energy during the entire period of internment. The women, including those from the upper classes, are credited with having curbed the spread of infectious diseases by their scrupulous cleaning. Since certain types of lice were carriers of typhus, every effort was made to eradicate them. Bedbugs, as well as the overcrowding mentioned earlier, prevented a decent night's sleep. Several women write about moving their mattresses outside into the corridors where they had more room to do battle with the bedbugs. In the following poem Dormitzer reveals a lighter side to her usually serious style of writing:

> *The Night of the Bedbug*
>
> Among the numerous torments here

58. *Drei Jahre Theresienstadt*, p. 63.
59. *Der Führer schenkt den Juden eine Stadt*, p. 48.

None arouses such fear
As the bedbugs which turn night
Into a hell of unknown spite.
Once day's burden is over
We search early for the bedcover,
Relax and say 'O man
Now Theresienstadt can . . .'
Quick to sleep, to private grief,
Dreams of home, its days of belief:
Now right now we try Verumon,
Sedormir, Pyramidon . . .
Drink Quadronox by the bucket
And still mutter 'Dammit'.
For on the dot of ten
You have battle with the bugs who love men,
Itching, biting you squirming, pounding—
If you can swipe at twenty
An army of a hundred makes work for plenty.
'What to do?' says Zeus—it's not a prayer
You shake your bed outside in the square.
Another filled with loathing
Pours around his cell exploding;
A third just devours his bread
His neighbour wants to plug himself with lead
The problem makes you swarmy then barmy:
How to wipe out the bedbug army.
The solution boils down to a simple case.
It will be alright when we're out of the place.
When we're back as good as home mice
Then goodbye to bedbugs, fleas, and lice![60]

Dormitzer enlarges on the theme in her memoirs.

The vermin in every building were intolerable (fleas, lice, bedbugs, the latter in unimaginable numbers—in one night I personally killed 103 of them in my bed, forty to fifty on the wall every
morning and slept for many weeks on the stone floor in the
corridor because it was more tolerable there). The plague of lice
was energetically confronted because typhus was carried by it, the
procedure for delousing being among the most unpleasant experiences. The extermination of bedbugs was impossible for they had

60. *Theresienstädter Bilder*, pp. 16–17.

invaded the hospitals just as much as the other buildings; the only way to have destroyed them would have been to set Theresienstadt alight at all four corners.[61]

In another part of her memoir Dormitzer describes the medical problem caused directly by vermin and proceeds to describe other typical camp diseases.

From the middle of April 1944, I spent ten weeks in the barrack belonging to the surgical wing of the hospital E VI, suffering from a nasty carbuncle on the back of my head. . . . The carbuncle I was suffering from had been caused by a vermin infection[62] (bedbugs) and had to be operated on several times by a Czech doctor who did not have any proper bandages and had to use paper and cellulose. Along with that and the general conditions the healing process was considerably slowed down. In my ward there were twenty people; both doctors and nurses were well qualified. Almost all the nurses were deported to Auschwitz in the autumn of 1944. One patient had a particularly nasty phlegmone on her arm and even Commanding Officer Rahm came to have a look at it. One day our room had to be cleared within two hours, because they needed room for twenty-seven patients with hip fractures. These kinds of fractures were very prevalent in Theresienstadt among the elderly and were attributed to the lack of vitamin D.

Coming only a few months after my husband's death, my will to live was weakened considerably during this illness and an abysmal indifference to everything overwhelmed me. My sister, who had recently arrived in the camp from Westerbork, was able to pull me out of this lethargy.

At one point a middle-aged woman was admitted who refused to take any food because she did not want to live. All efforts to care for this sick woman and to change her mind were futile. She starved after eight days; she had literally not touched food or drink.[63]

Tuberculosis took a heavy toll on the camp population as Kramer's account shows. She provides additional information about distinguished camp inmates.

61. Dormitzer, 'Leben in Theresienstadt', p. 2.
62. Eisenkraft maintains that people were literally eaten alive by lice. *Damals in Theresienstadt*, p. 47.
63. Dormitzer, 'Erlebnisse in Nürnberg', pp. 3–4.

After about three months I was allowed to work as a doctor and was assigned to the 'Genie-Kaserne', in particular to the TB ward. This also meant that I received somewhat bigger food rations. Although Theresienstadt was considered to be a privileged camp, the nourishment was so inadequate that I still suffered from malnutrition and hunger oedema. . . . Unfortunately not much could be done for those poor patients. In the large sick rooms there were many sufferers of tuberculosis. I tried to separate the infected ones from the others. There was a laboratory where the sputum could be examined. Here—among others—worked Dr Adler, wife of H. G. Adler who later wrote the most important book on Terezin. Both Adlers were sent to Auschwitz in 1944. H. G. Adler survived but not his wife.[64]

Work

Work was compulsory in Theresienstadt, except for the blind, the dying, the chronically ill, and the 'Prominenten' (most of whom, however, volunteered to work). Inmates were not only responsible for the maintenance of their living quarters, a task delegated and supervised by the room, barracks and block elders at various levels of command, but everybody also had to work an eight-hour day, that was increased in 1943 to a ten-hour day, seven days a week. All the memoirs refer to the grinding hard labour that further depleted their already malnourished and feeble condition. By the beginning of 1944 there were 1180 working women to every 1000 men.[65] There was an official work ethic for women: 'Now we demand discipline. She must work not only for herself but for the communal good.'[66] Her obligation beyond the workplace was also mandated: 'It is essential to generate a sense of the community in women, at least within their living quarters.'[67] The following list, taken from 1944 figures, shows the number of women employed in various jobs:

2600 in manual labour
1900 in workshops
1540 in nursing
1520 in housekeeping
1300 in administration
 620 in food services

64. 'Hell and Rebirth', p. 16.
65. See Adler, *Theresienstadt*, p. 416.
66. Ibid.
67. Ibid.

540 in supplies
510 in youth work
300 in agriculture
450 miscellaneous (107 doctors)
  63 saleswomen[68]

Many of the memoirs reveal positive perceptions of the working day, especially in terms of the camaraderie it engendered among women as they exchanged stories of their past existence and their hopes for liberation. One of the most touching memoirs is written by the blind woman Paula Frahm, who volunteered to work splitting mica, an essential war mineral used as an electrical insulator. It was mined by women.

> I soon realized that without useful occupation I would not be able to survive for long, so one day when an inquiry went round asking which blind people would like to work in mica production I was one of three who immediately volunteered. The splitting of mica demands not only a very sharp eye but also a very delicate sense of feeling and apparently they trusted us blind people with that. So there we sat on stools without support in the mica barrack at long tables for eight hours a day, with a lunch break, along with girls and women who could see, with our work in front of us and time to reflect and to tell stories.[69]

Later, when the mica barrack was closed, she knitted. 'By my work I protected myself from the worst deprivations.'[70]

Dormitzer's poem gives us a close look at the particular kind of pain inflicted on the women splitting mica

> *Mica*
>
> At four a.m. out of bed,
> At five out of the house,
> The darkness of rough paths.
> Hurry to the same place.
> No complaint, no murmurs.
> Mica calls, mica, mica.
>
> Two thousand women of any age
> Stand under the beast's whip,
> Pushed around, poked over

68. Ibid.
69. 'Theresienstadt von einer Blinden erlebt', p. 3.
70. Ibid., p. 4.

In long shifts of eight hours.
The air is bad, the room narrow
Because of mica, mica, mica.

Perched on a hard footstool
With no back—working, working,
Their backs crooked, aching,
Their hearts wildly, barely beating.
In front of their eyes, what a glitter:
That's from mica, mica, mica.

For sure the work is not easy
And if the quota is not reached
A new pain-atonement clubs you:
'You'll work an extra two hours as punishment',
A supervisor yells, a fierce beast
In the time of mica, mica, mica.

Countless victims collapse
In this grovelling, this torture chamber.
They cart them off on stretchers.
Death is drumming for them.
The last cry of the most wretched,
'My curse on mica, mica, mica'.[71]

Sternberg's memoir confirms Dormitzer's description of this suffering and adds a further dimension:

The work consisted of cutting with a knife thin strips from a block that was about 50 cm in size. The glare from the mica was so strong that after half an hour everybody's eyes were watering. After three or four hours our eyes were bleeding and we could only feel what we were doing, because seeing was now out of the question. I suffered so much from migraine and eye-bleeding that I dared to lie down in the 'Marotka'. This was the name given to the infirmary, where Czech-Jewish doctors fulfilled their duty sacrificially under the most primitive conditions. The danger in lying in the Marotka was that any day the command could come that all Marotka inmates were to go with a transport. In this case 'transport' meant being gassed in Auschwitz. In the jargon of the Czech SS, who guarded the camp, these Auschwitz transports were called 'selections'.[72]

71. *Theresienstädter Bilder*, pp. 18–19.
72. Alexandra Sternberg, p. 3.

Malvina Schalkova painted the mica-cutters at work (plate 7), and Eisenkraft tells us more about the splitting process and about its ultimate use:

> The mica slate was delivered in large blocks and was first broken up into small flat sheets in the so-called 'rough splitting room'. From there it was transferred to our barrack, the fine cutting room, where it was further separated into paper-thin, pliable sheets that could not be divided any more. All this was done with knives specifically made for the purpose, shaped flat like letter-openers. Because mica, which can reach a high temperature without burning, was used to insulate electrical appliances, predominantly in the aircraft industry, our workshop was considered important to the war effort.[73]

Generally speaking the traditional role of woman as cook, cleaner and nurse extended into the camp system, which essentially lasted until the mass transports of 1944 after which women also assumed much of the manual labour previously done by men. Women who had previously delegated cleaning chores to other women now cleaned for themselves and others, and, as mentioned earlier, did a commendable job washing down the latrines. Women's work squads also cleaned the barrack where the so-called prominent people lived but the only benefit it gave to the shabby little rooms was hygiene. Some jobs break the stereotype; Sternberg, for example, was transferred to the carpentry shop to work as a cabinet maker. She writes: 'Here we built coffins, not for Jewish people but for the guards and their dependents. We did not need coffins.'[74]

During Glas-Larsson's internment in the Little Fortress she put her skills to good use in a daring incident. This is how she remembers it in an interview recorded in the late 1970s:

> Once more we had been assigned to outdoor work. I was wearing blue trousers from home and a white shirt. I was not able to bleach my hair because water was not available. But we were working out of doors and Frau Rojko, the commander's wife, was counting us. She looked at me and said: 'And what kind of trade did you learn?' I'll never know where I got the nerve. I stepped forward and said, 'Frau Kommandant, I am a beautician, and I think a treatment would do you good'. At first she looked at me,

73. *Damals in Theresienstadt*, p. 38.
74. Alexandra Sternberg, pp. 3–4.

speechless, then, 'Where did you learn cosmetics?' 'In Prague.' 'What do you need?' 'A little vaseline and some lard. A little butter would do, or even grease.' That's exactly what I said, 'And an egg and some flour, so that I can give you a face mask.' I gave Frau Rojko a facial—in Theresienstadt. . . .

Because of this my situation in Theresienstadt was very good, for Commander Schmidt's wife also came. They had obviously talked it over together. So I gave her a facial too.[75]

After Theresienstadt Glas-Larsson was deported to Auschwitz and occasionally had further opportunity to use her skills there.

Old people made up a large proportion of Theresienstadt's population and many of them fell victim to the various diseases that were rampant in the camp. Medical staff were therefore in high demand and though supplies were scarce and conditions primitive, they worked long hours and provided some degree of comfort to sick people.

According to the memoir of an anonymous Viennese doctor there where 527 practising physicians in Theresienstadt of whom, according to Adler, 107 were women.[76] One of the these doctors was a woman named Wygodzinsky who was there from the summer of 1942 until her death two years later. This seventy-three-year-old woman is described in a letter by Frieda Sington as having been 'indefatigably active' during her interment.[77] Green's reference to the same woman certainly confirms the reputation of selfless dedication.

Mrs Ahlfeld-Schlesinger, a native of Cologne who spent two years in Terezin, recalls working as a nurse for an elderly physician Dr Martha Wygodzinsky. Dr Wygodzinsky, a tiny, white-haired lady in her seventies, had been known in her native Berlin as 'the angel of Nordens'. She had run a volunteer charity hospital for unwed mothers. In Terezin, she made her rounds on swollen, crippled feet, ill with diarrhoea and the typhus that would eventually kill her.[78]

Outdoor work was sought after because it offered some opportunity for fresh air and sun during the warmer months and in particular

75. *Ich will Reden*, p. 119.
76. Yad Vashem Archives (Jerusalem), 02/379, n.d., p. 3; Adler, *Theresienstadt*, p. 417.
77. Frieda Sington, letter in Yad Vashem.
78. *Artists of Terezin*, p. 88.

the occasional opportunity to steal vegetables or, as Eva Herskowitz reports, to smuggle vegetables into the ghetto and exchange them for bread.[79]

Although formal education was strictly forbidden, the women who looked after the children in the children's barracks made valiant and clandestine efforts to teach them, especially by means of art and music. Many, however, remained untaught and illiterate, as the following excerpt from Dormitzer's memoir shows. It also describes another kind of work that women engaged in.

In the post office I made a comprehensive catalogue of all deported people and those working outside the camp: name, place of birth, transport number and the most recent address in Theresienstadt were entered. On SS command this catalogue had to be destroyed towards the end of the war, so that it could never be determined how many thousand inmates Theresienstadt had seen. Every day I had to work my way through the so-called 'Avisos'—the recording of packages and other mail; it could entail 168 pieces of mail a day. The so-called 'package sluice', i.e. the examination of packages for forbidden contents, was carried out at that time by Czech policemen and Jewish ghetto guards, all of whom conducted themselves with integrity. Yet I never saw any SS officials in the office of the postal service. They once requested me to make use of the services of two boys, who must have been around twelve or thirteen years of age and were having problems. I gave them a pile of cards, which one was supposed to arrange alphabetically and the other then to number consecutively. After a while, when nothing had been done, I had to conclude that they knew neither the alphabet nor how to count. I sent the two of them outside into the courtyard to play and never saw these two 'helpers' again. That epitomizes the neglect of children in the most primitive, elementary knowledge, because instruction of children was strictly forbidden.[80]

Women who were by training and profession doctors and artists performed a variety of jobs that sometimes increased their chances for survival, as the following two excerpts illustrate. Dinah Gottliebova worked in the art shop in Theresienstadt, but also had the following assignments: 'I spent a lot of time at the stables painting horses, some for the foreman, Karl Klinger, and for his friend, Karel

79. Eva Herskowitz, letter in Yad Vashem.
80. 'Erlebnisse in Nürnberg', p. 5.

Pollak. The SS then ordered copies, which I produced with apelike speed. This earned me status and more lucrative jobs like fruit picking and herding sheep.'[81] Gottliebova was transported to Auschwitz on 8 March 1944. She and her mother survived.

Kramer gives the following report of her job description:

Like all other inmates I had first to join the so called 'Hundert-schaft' (group of hundred), that is to say to perform physical work. For some time I worked in a timber yard, then I had to dig potatoes. In between—together with three women doctors—I cleaned the office and bedroom of the notorious Eichmann, which was considered to be privileged work.

After about three months I was allowed to work as a doctor and was assigned to the 'Genie-Kaserne', in particular to the TB ward. This also meant that I received somewhat bigger food rations. Although Theresienstadt was considered to be a pri-vileged camp, the nourishment was so inadequate that I still suffered from malnutrition and hunger oedema.[82]

Zdenka Morsel was assigned to the most stressful job in the whole camp—typing transport lists. The following excerpt also shows to what extent these women lived by their wits and how essential mutual respect for property was under these conditions.

I was assigned to the cleaning detail, scrubbing halls, washrooms and toilets. Since I was a fast typist, two weeks later I was assigned to the Central Evidence Office, working the night shift. When there were no transports arriving or departing, we would work until 2.00 a.m.; when transports were leaving, we worked through the whole night.

The Germans demanded precise statistics, and we typed end-less lists, recording who came with each transport, who died, who left in each transport.

I lived in one room with twenty-three women, sleeping on triple bunks. I came to bed when the rest were off to work. I had to get up to clean the room and to fetch our bread rations. Occasionally I was ordered to unload potatoes or sugar beets, which were welcome chances to steal a few potatoes or beets for a meal. We also tried to steal coal or wood to cook, heat water for washing or warm up the room a little. The morale in our quarters was high,

81. Quoted by Mary S. Constanza in *The Living Witness*, p. 39.
82. 'Hell and Rebirth', p. 16.

and nobody would touch anybody else's food or property, such as it was.[83]

Mortality

This list of jobs performed by women must be projected against the tableau of sickness, disease and exhaustion, which were the typical conditions under which everybody, both men and women, were forced to work. In one case, recorded by Auerbacher, a woman's job and death fused one day, producing this recollection, surely one of the most horrifying in the history of Theresienstadt: 'Mama's first job in the camp was washing laundry from typhus patients. One day she found a very high stack of what appeared to be soiled sheets. As she tried to gather them up, she found to her dismay that they were dead bodies covered with sheets. People died like flies in Terezin.'[84]

Though eminent medical specialists from Berlin, Vienna and Prague looked after the sick their skills were powerless to confront malnutrition and, in the final year, the total lack of medicines. At one point the mortality rate was 150 cases daily. Dormitzer's poem 'Death in Theresienstadt' shows that even for a relatively healthy woman in her fifties death had become the reality she too could face at any time.

Death in Theresienstadt

Daily our faces grow gaunt and thin,
Water keeps bloating leg and limb.
Our breath begins to pant, short and anxious.
Nights are getting long, frantic.
Then death cries, 'Now it's come!'
Some poor soul ascends for home.
Not much to be done in requisition
The corpse is quickly placed in position:
A cover pulled over the head,
Whatever valuables left are quickly bled.
After two hours without sound or word-trace
The dead is shoved up to 'the good place'.
Twenty coffins stand there without names,
A day later they go to the flames;
Huddled together friends and relations moan,
Sob when they hear the Kaddish's solemn tones.

83. Quoted in *Women in the Resistance*, ed. Laska, p. 235.
84. *I am a Star*, p. 51.

Box by box, quick and terse
They begin their last journey in the hearse;
We look on until it goes from pity,
Return through the mud to the city.
The question inside each is fervent:
'When will they convey this servant?'[85]

Morsel's memory of attending her father's funeral confirms the description given in this poem: 'Several coffins were loaded on a pushcart and brought outside the camp for burial in a mass grave. The coffins were reused after each burial. I walked behind the pushcart carrying my father until I reached the gate; nobody was permitted to go beyond it.'[86]

Some women write about death with a spirit of defiant freedom. Two days before her death Grete Schmahl-Wolf had written two poems, both of which are now housed in the Leo Baeck Institute:

I am lying here in sick bay
On wooden boards to hold me.
My body's weak and skeletal
Buy my soul is free.

My limbs are weak from lying
In a body racked with needs.
Theresienstadt is where I am living
But my soul is free.

What I once was is forgotten.
I do not complain of what they took from me;
For I am reaching for the heavens
And my soul is free.

Another of her poem speaks of death in these terms:

Dying

Dying means nothing here
In these sad and gloomy rooms.
One stretch and you are free from hunger,
Hate and hopes and dreams.

Nobody weeps. Nobody prays.
There is neither touching nor mourning.

---

85. *Theresienstädter Bilder*, p. 20. The poem is printed in German in Appendix A.
86. Quoted in *Women in the Resistance*, ed. Laska, p. 235.

Just like a leaf that falls from its branch
Death has here no meaning.

Neighbours look with quiet calm
On the corpse with its doll-like wrapping.
Another death. So what?
And stolidly keep on eating.

They think. Good for him. Keep slicing
In case they miss a crumb.
Then the stretcher comes. That's what dying
Means in these sad and gloomy rooms.

Death became so commonplace that people were inured to it and viewed it as a release from the prevailing abysmal conditions. Some women died alone, like Glas-Larsson's cell-mate whom she refers to simply as 'Weil' and who was dying of cancer when they arrived at the Little Fortress. This is how Glas-Larsson describes Weil's death: 'Weil said to us, "Carry me outside so that I can see the sky and a tree." And that's the way she died and was buried— unceremoniously. So now there was one fewer in the cell.'[87] Eisen- kraft says that people spoke of death as casually as talking about stepping outside or taking a drink of water.[88] Death, in fact, appears to have been a less terrifying and threatening force than the fear of the transports. Suicide, though expressly forbidden by the SS, was a choice made by some. Ems has this to say: 'During these years it was neither a problem nor a major decision to take one's life, when faced with the indescribable fear of an unknown future, which almost everybody had. Many did so.'[89] And Auerbacher writes:

Under these terrible conditions, some people lost the will to live and took their own lives. A few days after our arrival in Terezin, my father saw a man starting to jump from an attic opening of the Dresden Fortress. Papa managed to grab the man's legs and pull him back inside. To his amazement, it was an old man from the transport. Papa spoke encouraging words to him and made him promise not to repeat this act. The next morning a broken body lay lifeless in the fortress courtyard. Papa identified him. It was the same old man.[90]

87. *Ich will Reden*, p. 117.
88. *Damals in Theresienstadt*, p. 16.
89. Hedwig Ems, p. 4.
90. *I am a Star*, p. 42.

A Viennese doctor (in an anonymous memoir) attributes the instances of suicides to the uncertainty that finally drove some people into insanity or to taking their own lives.[91]

Like other survivors of concentration camps, some people took their own lives later, after their release from Theresienstadt. These included the husband of Glas-Larsson (Georg Glas) who killed himself in Vienna at the age of forty-two, having survived both the Little Fortress and Auschwitz. Kramer also relates that some of the people on her transport to Switzerland later took their own lives.[92] The majority, however, opted to go on, both during their internment and after their release. Alice Bloemendahl characterizes the general attitude of camp inmates: 'Work, hunger, deprivation, danger, insecurity about what the next hour could bring and yet they went on living, living in a way that the enemy's cruelty could not destroy. They lived unbent and unbending, deriving their inner strength from spiritual, cultural and religious values and from the hope of a future. . . . That's how I perceived the Jews in Theresienstadt.'[93]

The choice, however, to go on living does not obliterate memories of a past life. These memories often skip over the harassments of the period after 1933 leading up to *Kristallnacht* and tend to linger in the Weimar period. A rich, fulfilled pre-Theresienstadt existence is often juxtaposed with present tortures in the form of 'before and after' pictures as in these three stanzas from a poem by Adele Strach, now in the Leo Baeck Institute:

> *Once and Now*
>
> Once an industrialist
> Now plateless
> . . .
>
> Once a lady-killer
> Now a coffin-bearer
> . . .
>
> Once well-housed
> Now deloused.
> . . .

Else Dormitzer's poem embodies similar contrasts.

---

91. In Yad Vashem Archives (Jerusalem), 02/379, n.d., p. 3.
92. 'Hell and Rebirth', p. 25.
93. 'Theresienstadt einmal anders', p. 4.

Then and Now

Once you were plump
Now you are skeletal,
Once you were a specimen
Now you are sick as a dog.
Once you had no cares
Now you have only problems,
Once you had good spirits
Now you suffer a useless fit,
Once you had a sunny outlook
Now you're a worm or a fox.
Once you ate in restaurants
Now you'd dine with Job,
Once you paid for everything
Now you'd steal anything,
Once they said, 'Have a nice day'
Now it's, 'Go jump in the lake',
Once you were involved with others
Now you're not even narcissistic.
Once you were depended on
Now you abandon anyone,
Once you were non-violent
Now you claw and tear,
Once you had beauty sleep
Now you prefer nightmare,
Once bankers greeted you
Now nothing under the mattress.
Once you were kissed
Now your lips won't move.
Once you were bourgeois
Now you're turned into Joe Soap.
Once you were so clean
Now you scratch and scratch.
Once life was a feast
Now it's not even a funeral. . . .
This list is what happens to you
At Theresienstadt.[94]

Eisenkraft describes one woman who arrived, 'blond, pretty, well-proportioned, well-groomed, gentle, good-natured and sociable'; after a year the same woman is described as 'stooped, un-

94. *Theresienstädter Bilder*, pp. 14–15. See Appendix A for original German.

gainly walk, neglected-look, coarse, vulgar, blunt, sullen'.[95] It is probable that the 'after' pictures of *all* the women share at least some of these characteristics. Many memoirs refer to a particular kind of walk, the 'Theresienstadt shuffle' that developed during their internment.

The most striking contrasts in 'before and after' pictures are found in memoirs that relate to the barrack that housed the so-called 'Prominenten'. The one oral formality that titled people retained from their past life was to address one another with such titles as 'Baron' and 'Countess'. Starke, a gifted writer with a sharp eye for poignant detail, has given us several outstanding portraits of prominent women in their Theresienstadt setting. Here is one set in the coffee-house:

> The uncurtained windows allowed the bright light to shine in. Our eyes, however, did not linger on the dirty, broken panes opposite but on the newly-erected, yellow construction on the corner of the wide townsquare which was hypocritically adorned with flower-beds. Coffee was served after a long wait, one did not have to serve oneself and there was a lump of sugar in the saucer. A woman from an exclusive Hamburg suburb . . . had sat down at our table. There she sat, shrivelled up from hunger and every kind of deprivation, reading with the same kind of matter-of-fact behaviour, as if she still were in the Alster pavilion.
>
> The afternoon sun brought out the soup stains on her dark clothing. I would have liked to remove the silver hairs that had fallen on her shoulders. The newspaper page was shaking in her delicate little hand. As she turned the page a well-formed louse, thrown off balance, hurried in great irritation from one line to the next.[96]

It is indeed merciful that women such as the one described here appear to have lost the awareness of how they were perceived by others. Personal care was certainly not a priority for any woman. There is a conspicuous absence of allusions to physical attractiveness or even the lack of it. Women were completely preoccupied with daily survival and beauty played no role in that. Morsel writes: 'Our clothing was threadbare, and we looked anything but attractive. No wonder the SS men did not molest us sexually. Besides, it was dangerous for them, since fraternizing with Jews was drastically

---

95. *Damals in Theresienstadt*, p. 35.
96. *Der Führer schenkt den Juden eine Stadt*, p. 126.

punished.'[97] The one exception to this was Glas-Larsson, who, as we saw above, indulged in a brief moment of vanity, when she bemoaned the lack of water, that prevented her from dyeing her hair.

Starke's memoir provides important information about the cultural background of some of these prominent women, whose lives at one time were linked with the leading literary figures of Germany. The following excerpt relates an incident that happened outside the barrack for the 'Prominenten' when Starke and the other cleaning women were on their way to work:

> In the garden-like courtyard there were the remains of a wooden folding chair from the cinema or church, no matter, a great luxury on account of its back. We sit down to wait. Suddenly I think I am having a vision. I see the Maximum Auditorium at the University of Munich. Large, public 11 o'clock lecture by Wilhelm Pinder, with slides, a very social event. In the first row, close to the middle entrance, an old lady sat through every lecture, treated by the professor with particular courtesy. Fine, black lace covered her reddish-blonde hair, dark glasses her eyes.
>
> 'There's Ernst Rosmer', someone whispered to me—a granddaughter of Liszt. She wrote the text of Humperdinck's *Königskinder* twelve years ago or more. Is it possible? But there is no question about it. Stepping out of the backdoor of a house in this little Bohemian town, feeling her way with a stick, came Elsa Bernstein, née Porges, mother-in-law of Gerhard Hauptmann's son Klaus—Ernst Rosmer.
>
> A black woollen headscarf covers her hair, now silver-white. the profile has remained unmistakably like Liszt's. We get up softly, make room for her and then we observe her sitting in the morning sun. Her blind eyes are unaware of the miserable surroundings and her thoughts are clearly lingering in the distant fairy-land of the past.[98]

Starke also writes about Mimi Mann, the divorced wife of Heinrich Mann, and describes her as 'the translator of Scandinavian writers . . . a tragic figure, whose spirit lingered in the past and sought security there. It circled around the Herzogpark in Munich and around the home and family of her brother-in-law Thomas Mann'.[99]

---

97. Quoted in *Women in the Resistance*, ed. Laska, p. 236.
98. *Der Führer schenkt den Juden eine Stadt*, pp. 47–8.
99. Ibid., p. 129.

Theresiendstadt housed many other women whose names were well known either on their own account or through their relationship to a prominent person. Johanna Broch, for example, mother of the Austrian writer Hermann Broch, was deported from Vienna to Theresienstadt on 14 August 1942 and died there on 22 December of the same year at the age of seventy-nine. The Austrian philologist Elsa Richter, who was born in 1865, and had won international recognition as an etymologist, was deported to Theresienstadt in October 1942 together with her sister Helene, a distinguished scholar of Romance languages and literatures. Elsa Richter was a pioneer in the field of phonetics and had penetrated academic territory unknown to women of her time. After the annexation of Austria she lost all her academic privileges and personal property. Both sisters died in Theresienstadt—Helene in November 1942 and Elsa in June 1943.

In all the hardships discussed so far in this chapter—the lack of food, long, hard labour—men and women received equal treatment. Regardless of how they responded, hardships were meted out with the same democratic rigour. In two vital areas the suffering of women assumed a specific, gender-related dimension. The biological clock of many women stopped in Theresienstadt, resulting in a cessation of menstruation, which caused their legs to swell and resulted in great discomfort for those who had to be on their feet all day. As many as 54 per cent of the women in Theresienstadt suffered from amenorrhoea for between three and seventeen months.[100] Women also had to face typical women's diseases. Starke writes about Alice Hansel-Haas, whose losses were overwhelming by any standard even before she had a mastectomy in Theresienstadt, presumably under crude conditions, even if the surgeon was skilled. Some years earlier her first husband had committed suicide, she had lost a young son to diphtheria and had already lost her remaining sixteen-year-old son and her mother to one of the transports. The one person left was her second husband, who had been separated from her when they reached Theresienstadt. Starke writes about visiting her in hospital.

'Just think', said Frau Hansel, who was lying near the window looking as transparent as a flower petal, 'the doctor recently asked my husband to come and see him. After a while I wanted to know what was going on. The two of them were standing so close to the door that I could hear what they were saying. When my husband

100. See Adler, *Theresienstadt*, pp. 522–3.

came back he found me and lifted me up. Now they have removed my breast. . . . Do you think my husband will be able to get over this? . . . When I am able to get up again, I'll have to go back to my quarters. There are rats there. You see, I am living at ground level in a shed with an open drain running through it. . . . I am so afraid of rats.' . . . . I do not think that Alice Hansel-Haas had to return to the rats. All her other worries were also to prove to be in vain. A short time later I saw her sister-in-law Mrs Kussy crossing the main street. She was carrying over her shoulder a fawn-coloured bag and was wearing a beautifully tailored tweed coat that was far too short for her.[101]

Appropriating the goods of someone who had died or had been transported appears to have been refined to quite an art, notably in the case of one woman in Hedwig Ems's quarters, who was always eagerly helping elderly women prepare their bags for transport. Since only minimum hand luggage was allowed, this woman was able to hoard a sizeable collection of goods which she then maintained had been given to her earlier as presents. (Officially all goods transported became the property of the camp.) Ems adds the uncharitable footnote, 'It didn't bring her any luck for she too was selected for a transport.'[102] Kramer's parenthetical reference to the same delicate subject is more sensitively framed. On packing for the Swiss transport she says: 'Soon the suitcase was packed. The few effects I had inherited from deportees—unfortunately all of us had to rely on such sad gifts—did not look too elegant.'[103]

Motherhood

The other gender-related area of women's suffering was motherhood. By Nazi decree there was no choice for a pregnant woman in Theresienstadt but to abort. The daily bulletin of 21 August 1943 carried a formal notice instructing doctors to abort all pregnant women, otherwise both parents would be transported. A further notice of 18 March 1944 warned room elders that they would be held accountable if a pregnancy were not reported. Adler gives a figure of 350 as the number of abortions but claims that there may have been as many as 230 births. Presumably these took place before the ban

101. *Der Führer schenkt den Juden eine Stadt*, p. 77.
102. Hedwig Ems, p. 10.
103. 'Hell and Rebirth', p. 22.

was issued.[104] Men presumably suffered the absence of their children no less than women, but since men did not work directly with children they were at least not reminded on a daily basis of their loss. Nor did they have to suffer the trauma of losing children with whom they had developed strong emotional ties. Of the 15,000 children in Theresienstadt, around 100 survived.[105] Here is a previously unpublished letter-poem, now in the Yad Vashem Archives, which was written by Ilse Weber, a highly regarded and published poet in Czeckoslovakia before she came to Theresienstadt. The German poem rhymes; I have rendered it here as a poetic narration.

> My dear boy,
> Three years ago to-day
> You set off all alone
> Into the world.
> I still see you in Prague
> Weeping at the window
> Of the train,
> Your brown curly head
> Leaning out,
> Begging me to let you stay.
> That we could let you go
> Seemed hard to you.
> For you were only eight,
> A little sensitive boy.
> When we came home without you,
> I thought my heart would break in two.
> Believe me, I have often wept
> And yet I'm glad you are not here.
> The stranger who took you in,
> She will surely go to heaven.
> I bless her with every breath
> My body breathes.
> You could never love her enough.
> Life is now so dismal here.
> They took away everything we owned;
> Our house, our country,
> Didn't leave a corner,
> Not a scrap

104. See Adler, *Theresienstadt*, pp. 524–5.

105. This is generally the figure given but Adler thinks it is too high. He estimates that in all there were no more than 10,000 children in Theresienstadt, of whom 8400 were murdered in the East. *Theresienstadt*, p. 573.

That once was dear to us.
Even your train-set
And your brother's little hobby horse.
They even took our name away.
Branded like cattle,
They drove us through the streets
With a number hanging round our neck.
I could bear it,
If I only were with your father
In the same house.
Even my little boy
Is not allowed
To be with me.
In all my life
I never was so alone.
You are still little
And scarcely understand all this.
So many of us are crowded
Into one room,
Body against body.
You bear the other's sorrow
And the pain of your own loneliness.
My little fellow,
Are you healthy
And are you learning
Like a good little boy?
I suppose you are not sung to sleep these nights.
Sometimes at night
It seems to me
As if I felt you lying close to me.
Just think, when we meet again,
We'll not know
What the other says.
By now you must have lost your German
There in Sweden.
And I cannot speak a word of Swedish.
Won't that be strange?
If it were only happening now!
And then I'll have a great big son.
Do you still like to play
With your tin soldiers?
I live in a regular barrack
With dark walls and gloomy rooms.

You barely see the sun
For all the trees and foliage.
I am a children's nurse here.
I love to help and comfort.
Sometimes I look after them at night.
The little lamp sheds a gentle light in the room.
I sit there and guard their sleep
And every child for me is part of you.
And then my thoughts go out to you
Yet I am glad you are not here.
Life has taken many precious things from me
And you have given me
Such happiness.
But I am willing to bear it,
Hard as it is.
You have been spared a lot of ugliness.
And I would gladly suffer a thousand agonies,
To pay for you a happy childhood.
Now it is late and I must go to bed.
If only I could see you
For just one moment.
But I can only write you letters
Filled with longing
And they will not be sent.

Weber and her remaining child later perished in Auschwitz. Hanoch Weber, the boy addressed in this poem, is now living in Holland and writes poetry.[106]

Another letter-poem, also in the Yad Vashem Archives, was written by a blind woman Regine Krampel to her thirty-six-year-old son on the occasion of his birthday. He had been released from Dachau and was living in England. Though written to a grown man, the poem is framed in affectionate, effusive language, filled with optimism that they will meet again.

My dearest son,
You still have not received my letter
And everything within me longs for you.
You are indeed used to having a party
Given by your dear old mother.
Thirty-six years have passed and gone

---

106. Henry Marx, 'Im Angesicht des Todes', *Aufbau*, 28 February 1986, pp. 8–9.

Since I laboured at your birth.
And many a tear I have shed
When my little darling was sick.
I could not give your childhood much,
In terms of fun and joy
For by the time you were ten
Your little mother was already blind.
Thus life went on
And picture after picture formed a chain
Of cheerful patterns
Etched in storm, sun and rain.
Twenty-three years passed
When suddenly one day
It happened on the street.
You were lifted and sent away.
I waited through the night for you.
Made sure your bed was made.
Your father stayed awake all night.
Outside an autumn storm was raging.
After fourteen days a card arrived.
From Dachau. You wrote you were well.
We should not wait for you.
You were healthy and in good hands.
For five months we bore the sorrow.
You came back but in what shape
. . . Heart against heart,
Beating together. Yes, my son.
You were in good hands.
We cared for you,
Snatched from death you flourished once again.
Our doctor did his best to make you well.
Our heavenly Father listened too.
And then you set off on your travels
And fled from danger's threat at home.
Freedom soon will call your parents,
I know for sure: You'll come back, my child. . . .
And now we have come to Theresienstadt.
We were sleeping in the damp cellars.
They took all light and air from us.
Were our ashes so precious here?
But a beam of light fell into our night
So please, don't be sad, my child.
A guardian angel looked out for us,

Sent by God, because your mother is blind.
And now we live in a big house
Protected from the worst hardships.
Many blind go in and out
And all call out and beg for bread.
I have described Theresienstadt, my son,
And nothing has meanwhile changed.
I suppose that Spring is pressing
Towards summer's full reward.
Could you please write soon to me
From England's shores.
I feel the thrill and pulse of joy
That you will come back to us soon.
And your birthday will give us again
The highest joy on earth.
Then our pain will be all in vain,
For you as well as for us.
Our warmest wishes accompany you
Wherever you go, my son.
God will lead you to the mother again
Who kisses you with so much love.
Your little mother Regine Krampel
Theresienstadt, 7th May 1943.

Birthdays, in fact, appear to be the catalyst for other poems, including one written by Regina Auerbacher to ten-year-old Inge. Inge Auerbacher is one of the few child-survivors of Theresienstadt and is now a successful writer living in New York City. Oestreicher's poem for her daughter Anna (Annchen) is filled with the pain of a seven-year separation. Anna Stamm's poem for a son who perished is a lament entitled 'Where did my child's last sigh go?' She writes of one dream in which she hears him comfort his mother, but in another dream she sees his blood-stained hands vainly reaching out for her's. Berta Anders, an Austrian woman, tells a touching story about a birthday present she received from two little boys for whom she had cared in the sick-bay and became, by all accounts, a surrogate mother.

Two of the children received special attention from me, Tommi and Klaus. Every week children received three decagrams of sugar and these two little fellows had been saving their sugar so that they could give me a birthday present. Can you imagine? A child—giving away sugar? Of course I didn't take it. They really

loved me. In the evenings I used to sit with them and often I
didn't even go home. I used to tell them stories. They asked me if
things were going to stay that way. And what it was like in the real
world. What could I tell them? After all, I had the feeling that we
would never make it out of there.[107]

Eisenkraft's memoir, though less harrowing than the poems, speaks
with simple sorrow of the agony of missing her children: 'Whenever
I lay on my miserable bedding or queued for the pathetic little bowl
of food, I saw in my mind's eye my two children standing before me
with sad eyes, calling out their last goodbye to me. . . .'[108] She is
even able to put her own pain in perspective when she hears the
story of a doctor's widow, daughter of a High Court Judge in
Germany.

> Her situation was basically a lot worse than mine and far more
> hopeless; it was, in fact, the worst pain a mother's heart can
> experience, like being thrust through with a dagger. Her son had
> been so infected by vile Nazi ideology that he was ashamed of his
> mother. He had enlisted as a volunteer even before the outbreak of
> war. In his last letter to his mother he wrote that he wanted to
> purge on the battlefield the blemish on his family, namely his
> Jewish descent.[109]

Eisenkraft is careful to add, however, that this was by no means the
rule.

Auerbacher's poem 'An Angel in Hell' makes a fitting ending to
this Chapter. It celebrates the archetypal good woman and mother
in the story of Mrs Rinder, a Czech woman, who divided her son's
mattress in half and gave one half to little Inge when the Auerba-
chers arrived in the camp. Her extraordinary kindness and unsel-
fishness are captured in this simple little poem.

An Angel in Hell

We searched the dump for each potato peeling,
Stole from the dead without guilt or feeling.
Nothing seemed to change; time stood still,
Was there anyone left with good will?

107. *Ich geb Dir einen Mantel*, ed. Berger *et al.* p. 55.
108. *Damals in Theresienstadt*, p. 20.
109. Ibid., pp. 20–21.

To this planet of shadow and despair.
An angel came to give help and care.
One hand was clutched by her little son,
She wanted to mother everyone.

Through time she moved on unseen wings,
Bearing food and other needed things.
This stranger reached out with heart and hands,
Asking no thanks, or making demands.

Both would never leave the abyss,
Or be touched again by life's kiss.
I search my heart for an answer, Why, why?
Where was justice, why their sentence to die?[110]

---

110. Auerbacher, *I am a Star*, pp. 40–1.

3

Cultural Activities

DURING the two-year period between the autumns of 1942 and 1944 the inmates of Theresienstadt, both men and women, were caught up at some level in the process of the normalization programme, which was gradually developed into an ambitious embellishment plan. The living conditions described in the previous Chapter were the backdrop against which this programme was enacted. Other factors are also worth noting, for example, the average age increased dramatically and the predominant nationality changed from Czech to German. In September 1942 58,500 people were living in the town and 131 were dying daily. Even with this high mortality rate thousands were being sent to the East (18,000 during September and October).

It is essential to remember that the affairs of Theresienstadt were ordered, designed and directed from Nazi Headquarters in Berlin and were as much part of the Final Solution as the gas-ovens of Auschwitz. At no time did these ostensibly humane innovations reflect a change of heart in Nazi thinking or an alternative to mass genocide. Theresienstadt was a carefully designed camouflage both to divert elsewhere growing world attention to the existence of death camps and to provide a temporary, practical means of disposing of prominent European Jews, mostly from Germany, Austria and Czeckoslovakia, who had distinguished themselves in industry, the armed forces or the arts and culture. Their contribution to Austro-German life had been too significant and conspicuous to warrant mass and immediate eradication. In short, they were an embarrassing impediment to the execution of Nazi ideology.

The legacy of art and music from Theresienstadt has been well, if modestly, documented, considering the quality and sheer volume of material produced. It is an area that is still wide open to research, particularly in the area of women artists. The two artists whose work is represented in this anthology are Charlotte Buresova and Malvina Schalkova. Buresova worked in the 'Lautscher Werkstätte', a workshop that produced all kinds of artefacts from stuffed toys to leather goods, which the Nazis either kept for themselves or sold outside the camp. Unlike Buresova, Malvina Schalkova did not survive Theresienstadt. The focus of this book, however, is Theresienstadt's literary legacy, the neglect of which has not gone unnoticed.[1] One explanation for this may possibly lie with the survivors themselves. Adler, for example, though he carefully lists the kind of literature written in Theresienstadt is, as noted earlier, disparaging of its quality, attributing what he sees as its mediocrity to the lack of 'a certain inner distance', an essential quality for the producing of literature, he claims, except for the highly gifted. The concentration camp, he further argues, precludes the possibility of such objectivity. He has this to say about poetry:

> Creative writing demands a certain inner distance, in order to process the experiences of the camp, and thus a poet was at a disadvantage compared to the artists. The artist can copy in such a way that he is able directly to mirror the face of the camp. The poet needs superior knowledge of his subject, something that presupposes maturity and a lot of ability. Otherwise he remains focused on surface reality and only offers a report, an illustrative document that not only lacks skill in projecting reality but also objectivity and at the same time colours it too emotionally. Creative writing would then have only been possible in Theresienstadt beyond the daily uncertainties and external events or in a superior perception accessible only to mature artists.[2]

I am sure that the artists themselves, the few who survived, would disagree with this assessment. One wonders what Adler could possibly mean by 'superior knowledge' of the subject. While there are differences in the levels of narrative skills and technique in the literary documents, the perception of the reality they convey is singularly unanimous and furthermore reveals extraordinary emotional restraint, certainly in the case of Dormitzer. Adler continues:

> The immense, mostly lost, flood of these writings consists of verses. For the most part they are clumsy, dull rhymes, that testify to the will to live and to the boredom of their composers; there were, however, more ambitious attempts, even remarkable documents, though hardly works of art in the sense their authors wanted.[3]

The following poem by Gertrud Kantorowicz has been chosen as

1. *Terezin*, ed. Frantisek Ehrmann, Otta Heitlinger and Rudolf Iltis, p. 316.
2. *Theresienstadt 1941–1945*, p. 616.
3. Ibid., p. 617.

a sample of poety that does not fit Adler's description of 'rhyming sickness':

> *Daughter of the Day*
>
> And so you fade. The step of hours is halting.
> No laughter give its hem to our week's graveness,
> So you have learned to walk dark halls
> Where living light and flower can only flutter.
>
> Daughter of day! Now you withdraw
> And blindly follow the nobler call.
> Old woman, you who stud with stars the moment
> How silent we kiss the ringed hands.
>
> And cover you in folds of the scroll's silk
> Adornment—bird, reed and wood—
> Change reaches out to get you: its figure looms,
> Your mouth composed resists—and we revere.[4]

Research for this book has also shown that Adler's claim that people had grandiose ideas about their writings is unfounded, certainly with regard to women, whose memoirs and poems are invariably prefaced to the point of self-effacement with tentative, modest remarks. Trude Groag, for example, writes in the preface of her manuscript: 'Do not take the contents as literature but as the expression of the deepest assault that overwhelms me every time I recall these memories.'[5] The tone in the preface of Dormitzer's book of poems is strikingly unpretentious and suggests that she had agreed to publish the poems because of a promise made to her friends (see page 132).

Lederer makes the same negative contrast as Adler between the poets and the artists, claiming that camp realities eluded the former: 'While the poets ignored the realities of Theresienstadt the painters were acutely aware of them. Three men among them—Bederic Fritta, Peter Kien and Otto Ungar—were outstanding.'[6] Lederer adds the following psychological insight:

> It appears that the uncertainty of life in the Ghetto with its unpredictable pitfalls produced a mental climate closely resembling that of puberty. Hence, in the manner of adolescents, the

4. Printed in *An den Wind Geschrieben*, ed. Manfred Schlösser, p. 283.
5. 'Namen und Ortschaften in Erinnerungen der Frau Trude Groag', 1965.
6. *Ghetto Theresienstadt*, p. 128.

writers sought to perpetuate the fleeting moment in their poems, thus hoping to escape from the depressing past and the sinister future. The style of the writers was conventional; the older generation clung to the patterns established by the literature of the nineteenth century, while the younger poets paraphrased the well-worn Socialist catchwords of the twenties, contrasting an unreal world of liberty, fraternity, equality, and justice with their hated environment. Genuine and strong as were their sentiments, their poems were spiritless and conventional.[7]

The conclusion that Lederer comes to about poetry written in Theresienstadt is that it was trivial and immature: 'A great deal was written in Theresienstadt, mostly poetry, but the standard was mediocre. Though most of the writers and poets were adults, their works bore the mark of immaturity.'[8]

Though the remarks of Adler and Lederer may be helpful and appropriate in some cases, they do not serve the purposes of serious literary research and tend to drive literary documents of the Holocaust back even further into the obscurity of the archives, where the attempt to rescue them from amorphous, genderless anonymity becomes even more treacherous. Furthermore, their inherent value as documents of the Holocaust remains undiscovered in the filing cabinet.

There is evidence to show that even before the official recognition of the arts as a legitimate pasttime in Theresienstadt, people were writing, singing, producing and acting in plays and clandestinely expressing their innate gifts and interests.

When the official ban against such activities was lifted there was a veritable deluge of cultural activities. In the field of music the most famous representatives were Pavel Haas, Gideon Klein, Jan Krassa, Viktor Ullman and the conductors Karel Ancerl and Rafael Schaechter. Among the works performed were *The Bartered Bride*, *The Marriage of Figaro*, *The Magic Flute* and Verdi's Requiem. Camp bulletins, issued daily, show that women played major roles in these activities. Among the more prominent singers and musicians were, for example, Hilde Aronson-Lindt, the pianists Edith Kraus and Alice Sommer-Herz, and the violinist Martha Geißmar. More germane to this subject, however, is in the first place why women decided to write and secondly the degree to which they were affected as writers by the sanctioning of literary activities. The

7. Ibid.
8. Ibid.

following anecdote by Gerty Spies, telling how she first came to write, offers one of the more compelling pieces of evidence that writing was a strategy of survival and that the decision to take up the pen was shaped independently of the official sanction. Spies describes the despair that overwhelmed her one day while working in the mica barrack:

> In bitter defiance I looked at my boss, a prisoner himself and a good soul, who was responsible to the Gestapo for everything that went on in the mica workshop. Could he not help? Suddenly he was standing beside me, spoke to me and tried to comfort me. But my tears kept on flowing. It was useless. He sent me outside. For five minutes I was all on my own, leaning against a tree. I still think of that tree. A young fellow who was holding guard duty came down from the ramparts and wanted to know why I was crying. I told him I was homesick and wanted to climb up on the ramparts and take a look, just one look, at the road leading to the West. He was sorry but he could not permit that. He too comforted me—it would not last—one day—I wonder if he himself lived to that day?
>
> The weeks went by . . . suddenly from my deepest despair grew a flash of inspiration which rescued me: 'Why don't you try to write? . . . Your thoughts will then not grope their painful way back along the bitter path of homesickness. Every minute and second they will have to be focused and you will then be able to shape your pain into creations of your mind. You will not hear what is going on and what is being said. Only your body will be here.'[9]

Poetry readings and lectures on European literature and philosophy constituted a major part of the cultural programmes. According to camp bulletins Else Dormitzer appears to have been a regular speaker and Alice Bloemendahl lectured three or four times a week on European literature, especially the modern writers which included, for example, the work of Hesse. In her memoir, written from a refugee camp in Bristol, she says that there were lectures in Theresienstadt on Plato, Hegel and Kant and seminars on Faust. She further comments: 'Perhaps more than a few of them were called to be guardians of the best of the European past, architects of a future that was fit for people to live in.' Bloemendahl arrived in

9. *Drei Jahre Theresienstadt*, pp. 39–40.

Theresienstadt on 19 July 1942.[10] She immediately volunteered to work for the Leisure Activities, and describes her involvement, reading aloud to the elderly and the sick:

> My listeners, often seriously ill, lay pale agaist the pillow and listened, sometimes making an observation or expressing a special request. . . . I read in the Bodenbach Barrack for almost a year, mostly to the same patients. I started with 'Memories of Women' and followed with the *Novellen* of Pentzold, Fontane and anything I could lay my hands on, Heine's 'Rabbi von Bacharach' from the *Buch der Lieder*, etc. . . .
>
> The Leisure Time Organization was growing significantly and was being developed quickly and thoroughly. When the number of German professors of literature grew I specialized in lectures in the French and English language, on modern and on the most recent literature and art, especially Flemish, sometimes running lectures three to four evenings a week in foreign languages.[11]

The political and social implications of many of these activities eluded the SS, resulting in one of the camp's more pleasant ironies, the fact that many of the sanctioned cultural activities would have been censored anywhere else in the Reich. This was particularly true of the daring and often politically engagé plays whose stage settings could have been the creation of the most innovative avant-garde stage directors in Berlin. This is how one writer describes them:

> Most of the stages were located in barracks garrets, which in itself created a fantastic atmosphere. There were two-storey-high roof supports made of gigantic 150-year-old beams. Feeble rays from the spotlights gleamed spectrally through the dusty room, turned the rags hung on the rope into grotesque curtains, transformed the dirt into the cosy atmosphere of a stable. . . . Here the famous German actor Kurt Gerron had indeed a more authentic backdrop for his *Beggar's Opera* interpretation than he had ever had in Berlin.[12]

The SS made some pitiful attempts to underscore German racial distinctiveness by insisting, for example, that lectures on Jews in German literature be worded 'German-speaking Jews in literature'.[13]

10. 'Theresienstadt einmal anders', p. 1.
11. Ibid., p. 2.
12. Quoted in *Terezin*, ed. Ehrmann, Heitlinger and Iltis, p. 213.
13. Adler, *Theresienstadt*, p. 589.

Work was never interrupted for High Holidays but religious activities flourished and were integrated into the programmes in the form of lectures and Bible studies, but these were not so well supported as the cultural activities. Jacob Jacobsohn makes the following comment:

> The Hamburg Jews had brought their own scrolls of the Law, their own Ark curtains, their own Prayer Shawls from Hamburg: the Cantor of this community wore the famous, beautifully embroidered Prayer Shawl of the Hamburg Cantors and used the old Prayer Books which had once been used in the Hamburg Synagogue. I also remember a service according to Portuguese rites, and Friday evening services held in the court-yard of the house where I lived by old Rabbi Undorn. When the Club House of the Sokolowna ceased to serve as hospital and convalescent home, services were held there too—by order of the Nazi authorities. Early in 1945 the synagogue in the Magdeburg Barrack was renovated and redecorated by the Dutch painter Joe Spier, a gifted, many-sided artist, who had also to paint pictures for the SS Club House.[14]

Women were also involved in these activities which were at their peak by the late spring of 1943 and there is evidence that some women took the initiative into their own hands and organized meetings independently. Caro writes about how she came to set up a Zionist organization in the spring of 1942, shortly after her arrival in the camp:

> At this time we were not supposed to go out but the next day I walked past the Czech guards (there was not a Jewish guard and work committee until much later) to the Jewish Chief Elder, Jakob Edelstein, whom at that time I did not know. He directed me to a *Chawer* Lolo Drucker, one of the few survivors of this group, who also had been thinking along the same lines. He put me in contact with the Czech leaders of the Women's International Zionist Organization (WIZO) from Brünn and Iglau, who had been actually waiting for someone to contact them. Because it was really dangerous at the time, Jakob Edelstein at first gave permission for meetings involving only twenty people and in this way twenty former WIZO members got together. At that time I was the only one from Germany. Under my leadership we met

14. Jacob Jacobsohn, 'The Daily Life, 1943–1945', p. 15.

every Sabbath afternoon. From twenty the group grew to fifty, 100, 200, and in the course of time the WIZO Sabbath afternoons with their lectures were the spiritual centre of an active Jewish cultural life. Meanwhile the *Chawerim* also met for the same purpose. We formed a *Hanala* and under the leadership of the gifted and very promising young Rabbi Schoen from Prosnitz the whole programme was discussed.

There were seminars and classes, lectures on every facet of Jewish intellectual history. We pursued an intense course in the history of Zionism with all its related problems regarding Israel. After all Erez Israel was the hope for most of us, the idea, the belief that gives us the strength to bear the present for the sake of the future.[15]

Breslauer confirms the existence of these activities in her memoir and adds that she was encouraged by them.[16]

The expanding of the Nürnberg Race Laws brought to the camp an increasing number of spouses from mixed marriages, many of whom had been converted to Christianity. Clara Eisenkraft, one such convert, distinguishes with a bluntness uncharacteristic of her usually gentle prose between nominal Christians and what she terms 'conscious Christianity'. She rhetorically asks the Christians in the Reich where their conscience was when the Jews were being persecuted.[17] She writes fervently about the spiritual sustenance she received from reading the Bible and from meeting with other Christians, presumably the 'conscious' ones. She adds: 'We probably had a greater sense of worship than many urban congregations have in famous cathedrals.'[18] Eisenkraft strongly indicts formal Christianity and stresses the intimacy and comfort of her relationship to Christ, which appears to be independent of ritualistic underpinnings. She also singles out Baeck for his devotion to the spiritual and material needs of the inmates, a view shared by other women. Edith Kramer, for example, records the following memory of evenings with Baeck:

One of my patients was the sister of Rabbi Baeck. Unfortunately she died in the early days of my work in the Genie-kaserne. Her daughter, Nelly Stern, was also a doctor and worked in the same

15. Klara Caro, p. 6.
16. 'Erinnerungen an Theresienstadt, p. 9.
17. *Damals in Theresienstadt*, p. 32.
18. Ibid., p. 51.

building as I. We shared the duty in the sick rooms and helped each other. I liked her from the beginning and we became good friends. Nelly introduced me to the discussion evenings of her uncle, Rabbi Baeck. These meetings were held from time to time and usually six to eight people were invited. Each of them could choose a subject to lecture on. Rabbi Baeck conducted the discussion which followed. One could prepare oneself with the help of the library which was quite good. Rabbi Baeck would offer his final comments on the discussion. These used to be the highlight of the evening. He was so well-versed in all areas of science, art and politics that we were all quite enthusiastic about these evenings which belonged to the few bright spots in T.[19]

The clash of the image of Theresienstadt as a normal place to live, in fact as a ghetto of culture, and as a place of terror is exemplified by an event that took place on 13 November 1943. This event intrudes on the cultural programme and indeed on the routine of the inmates' daily grind as an ugly reminder that they are prisoners of a system that could annihilate them at any time. Virtually every memoir mentions it, many in great detail. Dormitzer wrote a poem about it. This was the notorious occasion when the Nazis forced all the inmates of Theresienstadt to congregate in a huge meadow outside the camp to be counted. With the exception of a few minor discrepancies on points of detail, there is general agreement in all the memoirs about what happened that day. Here is Breslauer's description:

It was a really dismal, cloudy November day and quite unsuitable for an 'excursion'. About 35,000 people were involved and the field was surrounded by soldiers. We were divided into groups and the most primitive kind of counting continued till night fell. Of course they could have counted us a lot more simply but that would not have been torture for the Jews, and that was the purpose of the exercise. When we were completely frozen to the bone the order was announced that we had to spend the night there. We were already trying to figure out how we could camp out there when suddenly the command was given to return. Many of us were thinking that the purpose of this expedition was to suddenly kill all of us. We breathed a sigh of relief and began to march back in pitch darkness—no simple feat for 35,000 people.[20]

19. 'As a Doctor in Theresienstadt', p. 6.
20. 'Erinnerungen an Theresienstadt', pp. 7–8.

Ems writes:

We proceeded at a snail's pace for other groups kept pouring out
of other streets, hindering us from moving forward. Meanwhile,
we heard continuous gunfire and indeed there is little doubt that
on that very morning many were shot in the Little Fortress.
Finally we arrived at a rather large terrain, presumably used for a
parade ground in earlier days; it was called the 'Bauschowitz
Basin'. There they divided us into groups of a hundred, men and
women mixed. Surrounding the area was a hilly incline on which
armed soldiers were standing. It was obviously hours before all
the camp internees were conveyed there. There was a total of
38,000 people, including women with babies in prams, as well as
toddlers. When everybody had been assembled the SS men went
round with whips and counted the individual groups and heaven
help the person who was missing, perhaps because he had stepped
out of the group, for whoever was in charge was given a thrashing.
Near me there was someone missing. Someone was ordered to
whip him. Then the SS man said: 'You call that a beating? I'll
show you what one is!' And then he gave the person a terrible
beating-up. In a group opposite me there were little children, for
whom keeping still was of course sheer torture and some of them
were playing in a circle. Suddenly an SS man came up to them
and was enraged at them; it's a miracle he didn't hit them. . . .
Suddenly at four p.m. the entire SS had disappeared and we
were left waiting for the order to go back. But nothing happened
and there we stood, helplessly. When nothing happened between
five and six o'clock we started moving en masse and marched
back, which was difficult for us on unfamiliar, bumpy terrain.
Meanwhile it had begun to rain. Then when we arrived at the
gate of the ghetto it was bolted and was not opened up by the
guards on duty and all this still in the rain. Our camp Elder,
Eckstein, finally managed to get through and after negotiating for
two hours at headquarters, received permission for the gate to be
opened. In the history of the Jewish people it is a credit that no
panic erupted, no child was injured, no pram overturned. When
you consider that there were 38,000 people who had set off on
their own initiative without leadership, of course, hungry and
weakened and because of the rain wanted to keep on moving. . . .
I got back at ten o'clock, the last ones not until around two in the
morning. The SS had not considered the possibility of the Jews
acting independently and their intention had been to simply
abandon us outdoors. How few would have survived a cold

Arrival at Theresienstadt (Malvina Schalkova)

Privileged accommodation for the 'Prominenten' (Malvina Schalkova)

Laundry tubs (Malvina Schalkova)

Kitchen work (Malvina Schalkova)

Rest (Malvina Schalkova)

Mealtime (Charlotte Bursova)

The mica factory (Malvina Schalkova)

Deportation – the Last Road (Charlotte Bursova)

Main Gate, Theresienstadt

Theresienstadt Courtyard

Aerial View of Theresienstadt

November night without food etc. on the cold earth is fairly obvious.[21]

Sternberg tells the purpose of the whole exercise:

SS men on horseback kept watch over this enormous array of people. All around the basin were pockets of soldiers armed with machine guns. Whispered rumours went the rounds. German fighter planes were circling over the basin. We all thought we were going to be bombed or that the basin was mined or that we were going to be shot collectively with machine guns. We stood in this painful uncertainty until ten o'clock in the evening without food or drink. Many people collapsed from agitation or exhaustion. They were revived with the butt-end of a rifle. We had to register forty dead that day. What emerged later was that this whole manoeuvre was for the purpose of a census. They wanted to determine just how many Jews in Theresienstadt there were still to be gassed.[22]

Adler's account coincides with these memoirs and includes a comment about the consequences of the day's excursion:

People kept on standing and were not allowed to step out of line to provide for their needs. It got colder and began to rain. The elderly and the children were getting cold and soaked to the skin. Soon it was dark and the hours passed. The crowd was now becoming more and more agitated and terrorized. Many could not take it and collapsed. No help was offered except between individuals. After standing for about fifteen hours, people were finally allowed to move on at 8.30 but nobody knew whether they could go home, for nothing was said and Mandler and his companions had disappeared. Nobody led the way, people panicked and pressed in a wild throng towards the only exit from the basin. It took several hours to get this mass of over 30,000 people back again. It was restrained to some extent by a few sensible guards at the exit point, now completely jammed, and a total disaster was thus prevented. The return to the town was only partially completed by 11 o'clock but many of the elderly and sick had stayed behind because they simply could not go on. In the darkness they had crept into a half-finished barrack ('Südbaracken'), had lain

21. Hedwig Ems, pp. 15–16.
22. Alexandra Sternberg, pp. 4–5.

down in their helplessness and fallen asleep. They had to be given shelter all night. Men with stretchers, who had passively looked on during the day and evening, now had a lot to do. This is the way the day excursion from the ghetto ended, for many thousands the only time they got to leave the camp during their years of internment.

The consequences of that dark day were heavy colds, pneumonia and other illnesses. Some died immediately or shortly after the census. The camp fell into chaos for several days; people were exhausted, work patterns were disturbed, the kitchens were not functioning properly and it took days for the bread distribution to start working again. . . .[23]

Lederer's account adds an interesting footnote to the failure of the whole exercise:

Several fatalities occurred on the drill ground, and many elderly people fell sick as a result of their exertions and died soon afterwards. It is estimated that altogether between 200 and 300 prisoners paid with their lives for the census. Since the object of the census had not been achieved a new count was held between 19 and 24 November. The prisoners had to hand in their identity cards and the SS compiled their own card index from them, thus finally arriving at a fairly reliable figure of the Ghetto population.[24]

The cadence of the original German in Dormitzer's poem (and I hope of the translation) captures the slow, ponderous march of starving people; verbs and nouns expressing inner anguish pile upon one another to convey an overwhelming sense of stress and terror. Her poetic diction powerfully evokes an atmosphere of dreary dampness in which she depicts the story of the census.

Census

Dense crowds proceed at dawn
Through Theresienstadt's still empty streets
Five abreast curving around corners into squares.
The beast checks if anybody has stumbled.
Tóday God's chosen people are being numbered!

---

23. *Theresienstadt*, pp. 160–1.
24. *Ghetto Theresienstadt*, p. 105.

You see each kind of person,
Only the sick are allowed to stay behind,
At five o'clock the order went out to herd—
No one exempted, into one place:
The lame lead the blind, everyone's excoriated.
Today God's chosen people are being recorded!

Mothers push prams,
Fathers carry puny sons.
The elderly drag along on crutches or just sticks.
The census taker begins his meticulous task:
The pale sun is peeled from the clouds and plundered.
Today the chosen people are being numbered!

Finally the counting place is reached!
In an arch we move across Bauschwitz earth,
No chair, no stone or bench to sit on.
No wall to lean your back on:
Stand in hundreds, the command to the frozen.
So today they can count more easily the chosen!

Basic modest needs plague us.
Hunger rampages through our stomachs.
Nothing hot is offered, not a drop of water.
Our faces grow pale and dribbly.
Frost and deprivation have us routed.
Today the chosen people are being counted!

Hour after hour slips by.
The bare earth is the only place to sit,
Despair and diarrhoea mix
And some pass out or pass on:
There we lie stretched out like the dead.
Today the chosen people are being read!

Night is like a corpse, no star in the sky!
Desperate, everyone asks the other:
'Will we stay here till tomorrow?'
Trembling, quailing, fretting, fainting,
Those usually brave find optimism numbered!

Finally the order barks: what relief,
'The Jew can go to the ghetto!'
Scurry, push, elbow, shove, curse;
And parents shrink towards children, children peer
For parents—again to quarters, nobody at play.

The chosen people were counted today![25]

The issue of survival in the concentration camp is a major theme in Holocaust studies but is a particularly thorny one with regard to Theresienstadt, because it was founded and run on the whole principle of deceit. Adler makes the following distinction between Theresienstadt and the other camps, notably Auschwitz:

> In Auschwitz sheer despair was supreme, and the reality of the situation was unambiguously recognized. Even if some vital, indestructible spark still flickered, or if a person could escape in spirit by some magical transformation into a more pleasant delusion, reality was nevertheless seen for what it was and basically nobody was deceived. It was not that way in Theresienstadt, where almost anything could be repressed, where illusion ran rampant and hope, merely dampened by anxiety, suffused everything that lay under thick fog. As soon as the normalization programme dazzled the prisoners with 'the beautification of the city', there was no place in Western Europe, not even in the Jewish ghetto camps, where camp inmates were more removed from reality than here. Truth occasionally emerged from the darkness, touched the people and after giving them a little scare, let them fall back again into their masquerade of living.[26]

Whether fortitude or self-delusion prevailed, or whether people knew or suppressed the truth about Theresienstadt, is essentially less important than the fact that for the most part people somehow managed to go on living and some women, as the following excerpts from their memoirs will show, were certainly not fooled all the time. Breslauer writes about the coffee-house: 'It was a relaxation for us to sit on proper chairs at tables with flowers and be able to forget our misery for a while. Music and lively lectures took care of our entertainment and it was possible to have a conversation with a friend for an hour in decent surroundings and not have to sit or squat on the edge of the bed.' Speaking of the introduction of these new facilities she continues: 'If all these facilities rescued people momentarily from their misery, they were in fact only moments, which could not delude us about the seriousness of our situation and about the dangers that threatened us.'[27]

25. *Theresienstädter Bilder*, pp. 11–13.
26. Adler, *Theresienstadt*, p. 158.
27. 'Erinnerungen an Theresienstadt', p. 9.

Dormitzer has this to say:

> Whenever a foreign commission was announced, Potemkin villages were set up, i.e., there were increased rations, all sorts of lovely things came from Prague and were distributed to us, the inhabitants had to walk through the streets well-dressed, anyone who had nothing decent to wear had to stay at home and the children played happily on playgrounds made for this purpose. There were beautiful displays in the shop windows but none of the goods were for sale. It is fortunate that some of the foreign delegates noticed how things really were. Needless to say none of them ever saw the squalid quarters but only some of the renovated rooms furnished for the purpose. In the same genre a propaganda film was produced for neutral countries: 'Hitler gives the Jews the Present of a Town'. While none of us ever saw a river there (we were not allowed to leave the ghetto) a swimming pool was set up on the river Elbe outside the city with amusing bathing activities; bathing suits and beach wear came from Prague. There was dancing in the café or outdoors. The post office was extremely busy with mountains of packages being delivered and letters distributed, whereas in reality numerous packages were stolen by the Nazis and a strict check was carried out when every parcel arrived in the presence of the recipient before part of it was taken as contraband.[28]

As noted in Chapter 1 the culmination of the plan to normalize and embellish the town occurred on 23 June 1944 when the International Delegation of the Red Cross arrived to visit. It had never looked more attractive, though no doubt the embellishment was in direct proportion to the physical degeneration of the inmates, whose skills and manual labour had accomplished the transformation. Working from statistics of those who were recorded as sick during this period, Adler points out that the more they embellished the place, the more sensitive to disease the inmates became. For example, on 16 February 1943 31.3 per cent of the inmates were officially sick.[29] The following excerpt describes the role artists were forced to play in preparation for the international delegation:

> When the neutral country inspection teams came to check on how 'humanely' the Nazis were treating the prisoners, the artists had

28. Dormitzer, 'Leben in Theresienstadt', p. 4.
29. Adler, *Theresienstadt*, p. 510.

one week to facelift the dismal camp. Leo Haas described how they had to paint the fronts of buildings, the railroad station, and make street and other signs (such as 'Ghetto School', 'Synagogue', 'Restaurant'); fake posters announcing events that would never take place on billboards that did not exist previously (and would be taken down immediately after the inspection); dress up shop façades on the outside and make up displays for the inside to make them look used and patronized. All buildings along the route that these inspectors would take were refurbished.[30]

One inmate was even called upon to take up a new interest for the day. An Austrian woman recounts the incident:

One day visitors were announced, from the Red Cross or some kind of delegation, so that people could see that all those rumours were not true. So thirty to a room were now reduced to fifteen and the rooms were nicely furnished. A dental surgery was set up with a real dentist. Chess-players were put in a room. My father had never played chess in his life and now he had to play all day until the delegation arrived.[31]

This is how some of the women described the visit of the delegation:

Children, decked out in finery taken from the clothing room, had been taught to address the camp commander as 'Uncle Rahm'. Young girls in white aprons offered them sandwiches on trays, made from sardines from the Portugese firm Sam Ammon, which had been confiscated from parcels. The children had to decline with the words: 'Not sardines again!' That's the way Irma Zancker, who had to be there, described the scene.

The day passed, a day on which we had pinned so many expectations and passionate hopes. The opportunity had been squandered. The actors of this drama had another three months. But nobody knew that at the time.[32]

Klara Caro goes as far as to accuse the delegation of being in collusion with the Nazis:

It was never clear to me to what extent the so-called commission

30. Quoted by Mary S. Constanza in *The Living Witness*, p. 28.
31. *Ich geb Dir einen Mantel*, ed. Berger *et al.*, p. 63.
32. *Der Führer schenkt den Juden eine Stadt*, p. 131.

was in league with the Nazi criminals. If it had been a serious commission who really wanted to investigate our living conditions, then they would have examined more than the façade built for the purpose and would have gone independently into the stables and attics. They on the other hand only saw what the Nazis showed and presented them, so that little children, for example, were drilled to call 'Uncle Rahm,' (the cursed name of the last CO, unfortunately still at large) 'we don't want any more sardines', to give the impression of being well nourished.[33]

Regardless of whether or not Adler's assessment is correct, we can still conclude that the activities during these two crucial years were powerful expressions of resistance and that women played a major role in them. Lederer sums it up well: 'In giving their blessing the Germans certainly did not foresee the wide scope and intensity which cultural activities would assume in the Ghetto. They did not imagine that an institution intended to further their fraudulent propaganda would become the focal point of artistic achievements, and a weapon of spiritual and intellectual resistance'.[34]

Art became an essential part of the life of the Ghetto. To the older prisoners it was a source of consolation, helping them to forget the dreary present and to conjure up happy memories of the past. To the younger prisoners it was an inspiration, a source of strength and courage. Jacobsohn offers this balanced viewpoint:

But it would be unjust to blame the people for using those institutions and, by using them, helping the Nazis indirectly to carry out this manoeuvre of camouflage and deceit.

Anyone who has lived through the days when large transports to the East left Theresienstadt (as I did in September and December 1943), who has seen the hurrying, bewildered masses of humanity, anyone who has witnessed those days of horror and despair will understand that the small pleasures of life were essential to counterbalance this misery. Just because the danger of deportation was menacing everyone at every moment, the people in the Ghetto had to live as if this danger did not really exist, as if a life of freedom and human dignity was waiting round the corner for those now banished behind the walls of the Ghetto.[35]

---

33. Klara Caro, p. 19.
34. *Ghetto Theresienstadt*, p. 125.
35. Jacobsohn, The Daily Life, p. 12.

In September 1944 a woman arrived in Theresienstadt whose presence was essentially far more significant than the highly publicized delegation a few months earlier. She was of course admitted to Theresienstadt as a number, but her real identity was Ilse Blumenthal-Weiss, a respected poet, and correspondent with Rilke in the twenties. She arrived in a transport from Westerbork with her husband Dr Herbert Blumenthal and their daughter Miriam. They had already lost a son in Mauthausen.

The harsh rigours of Theresienstadt were mitigated for her to some extent by her friendship with Rabbi Baeck whom she had known previously. She describes the time she spent with Baeck as 'hours when all terrors, fears and deprivations did not appear to be present. For at no time, at no time at all, did we ever speak of the dreadful situation in which we found ourselves'[36]. She credits Baeck with having taught her that it is possible, even under the most oppressive conditions, to remain true to the real values of life. Furthermore, sensing in her deprived spirit the need for privacy, he arranged for her to use the room of a friend for a few hours every week so that she could have the solitude she needed to write.

It is indeed curious that though the reputation of Theresienstadt is linked to cultural activities, the writings focus far more on privation than on the provision of culture and learning, historically an essential element in Jewish life. (The census memoirs are proof of this.) Though the cultural activities had peaked by the autumn of 1944, Blumenthal-Weiss's insight into this aspect of Theresienstadt in the poem 'Variety Evening' is as succinct a commentary as one can find. It illuminates the reality behind the theatrical Theresienstadt pose, unmasks the irony behind the façade and with consumate skill plays with the literary irony in the first and last stanzas with its obvious allusion to the Heinrich Heine poem 'Der Vorhang fällt', reminding the reader of Heine's exile from another German audience in the nineteenth century.

Variety Evening

It's curtain time: faces change to poses
Before an audience acting like it's home.
On stage they dance and sing and twirl
And kill the sadness with the theatre's wings.

---

36. *Begegungnen mit Else Laskes Schule, Nelly Sachs, Ilse Blumenthal-Weiss, Martin Buber* p. 22.

The masks are real. They're made from verses.
The moonlight too that rests on nearby hills.
That too they think is real. And so they drift
To no man's land, hemmed in by hope and memory.

And do not see that picture and the shadow
Are the same. That all the players muffle mist.
That in the glow of noble deeds on stage
Players doomed to die are fighting just to live.

The curtain falls: on empty floorboards
Vermin keep on eating mind and limb.
To-morrow's dawn will bring another call
To stagger towards the slaughter-rail for transport.[37]

---

37. *Mahnmal*, p. 24. The poem is printed in German in Appendix B.

4

Transportation and Liberation

UP to now I have been dealing essentially with the mass deportations *to* Theresienstadt during the period from November 1941 to the autumn of 1944. Transports *from* Theresienstadt constitute a separate and even more painful subject, and relate to the central anguish of the camp against which all other hardships and deprivations pale. Selection procedures for transport lists appear to have been arbitrary, though knowing the right person spared some people, at least for a time. Ernestine Luze recalls how her friendship with a Czech woman whose husband had some authority in the camp saved her from a transport list. She hid for two days in her room until danger passed. Called once more for a later transport, it was her mother this time who saved her family. She recalls: 'The SS man was standing behind a podium and my mother—a little wisp of a woman like myself—goes up the steps and says: "Please, let us stay here." Can you imagine? He was so confused . . . "Please let us stay here! Look, my daughter is working and my husband is too. Leave us here. Cross off our names!"'[1]

The terror of the transports invaded the consciousness of every inmate, reminding the most optimistic and resilient of the futility of his or her existence. Dormitzer describes a December transport:

> *Transport*
>
> *The sluice is the place where those arriving and*
> *departing were thoroughly searched and stripped*
> *of their possessions*
>
> Running, whispers, anxious questioning
> In drab December days,
> Here a querulous complaint, there quiet quavering,
> A whole city is on its legs,
> In every mouth a single expression stays:
>   'Transport!'

1. *Ich geb Dir einen Mantel*, ed. Berger *et al.*, p. 65.

An icy wind blasts street and shed,
They call out: 'Get your bread!'
Flapping of washing, rolling up of beds,
Grasping of rucksacks, then a moment's truce
With friends before setting off for the sluice,
    'Transport!'

Now is the time for last looks,
A glance, a handshake: 'Farewell!'
One is standing with his scythe,
He is not waving, he is for the ride,
He'll move from camp bell to camp bell.
    'Transport!'

A call, a whistle—flapping of jackdaws
When will the next ones get off?
Is this the law for us? They know no laws.
When will our redemption come? Is this our measure?
Protect us, You, our treasure, from the TRANSPORT.[2]

The transports of the autumn of 1944 demolished the camp
hierarchy, obliterating all distinctions between the 'Prominenten'
and ordinary inmates, taking even the Jewish Elders and their
families and most of the artists and musicians whose talents had
shaped the cultural activities. The word 'transport' is more than
synonymous with Theresienstadt; it is a metaphor for the camp
itself, aptly named elsewhere the 'anteroom to Hell'.[3] The word 'gas'
had been introduced to the camp in August 1943 by the children
from Bailystock but the primary fear that it evokes in the women's
memoirs is of the unknown, rather than a specific threat. In fact, it
was a worse threat than death itself. It is often asked how much the
transportation victims knew as they were herded towards Auschwitz. The Theresienstadt women often express gratitude that they
did *not* at the time know the implications of the word 'Birkenau'.

Gerald Green, though, relates an incident which indicates that
information about the fate of a transport was at least in one case
transmitted back to Theresienstadt.

Not every inmate of Terezin was deceived. A woman I met in
New York, whom I shall call Mrs Ruckmann, showed me one of

2. Dormitzer, *Theresienstädter Bilder*, p. 8. The poem is printed in German in
Appendix A.
3. *Terezin*, ed. Frantisek Ehrmann, Otta Heitlinger and Rudolf Iltis, p. 127.

these Birkenau cards dated 25 March. It had been sent to her from her sister at Birkenau. Before leaving Terezin Mrs Ruckmann's sister had told her: 'If my writing slants upward it will mean everything is all right. If it slants downward it means we are going to die.'[4]

It slanted downwards.

The most monstrous aspect of the transports was the manner in which they were organized. People were awakened from sleep in the middle of the night and taken to the 'Schleuse', where they were processed for departure. Else Dormitzer describes what happened as follows:

> The worst horror of all were the transports to Poland which included the old and the young, the sick and the healthy, those who held the best jobs as well as those who were not able to work. The summons came in the middle of the night; those thus summoned had to go immediately with their luggage to the 'sluice' and could not leave there; they were taken by the police to the station along sealed-off streets and crammed onto freight cars. It repeatedly happened that their meagre pieces of luggage remained in the station because the CO, obviously on purpose, gave the departure order too soon. These transports were comprised of 1200 to 1500 people; the autumn transports of 1944 transported 15–20,000 people to Poland, among whom many were already dying. The transports were called workers' transports and their destination was supposed to be Germany. It is a mercy that those leaving and those remaining did not know that they were all actually going to Auschwitz and for the most part to the gas chambers.[5]

Morsel, who typed transport lists, tells the agony of her first-hand experience with departing transports:

> One transport was leaving after the other. By this time we were aware that the deportations away from Terezin meant no improvement. Some people selected for transports did not show up, some got sick, some disappeared into hiding. The papers accompanying the transports had to be retyped over and over again. In the chaos, the typists were ordered to the railway station, I among

4. Gerald Green, *The Artists of Terezin*, pp. 30–1.
5. 'Leben in Theresienstadt', p. 4.

them. While some SS men were loading our people into the box cars, marking them off the lists, others kept threatening to put us on the train if we did not type fast enough. By the time the train pulled out the few of us who were left behind were numb from cold and from fear, and I could never remember how I got back to my bunk.[6]

Caro calls the transports 'the separation of families, the destruction of the community, the way into the unknown and the start of yet another hard beginning'.[7] Paula Frahm, the blind woman, writes:

One night the light is turned on, everybody sits bolt upright out of sleep, the Room Elder is standing in the room and reads out a list of names of those selected for the next transport. The next day we see them again walking along with their cases heading for the designated meeting place, silent and oppressed, setting off on a pilgrimage to a fate whose magnitude we at that time still did not suspect. It was not till much later that we found out that most of them had been taken straight to their death in Auschwitz or in one of the other extermination camps.[8]

Käthe Breslauer was called for a transport and unexpectedly released. She describes what happened when she returned to her room: 'Back in our quarters again we were joyfully welcomed, as if we had returned from the dead and we had to tell our work companions all about our experiences in hell and purgatory'.[9] Gertrude Austerlitz was not as fortunate. After finding her name on a list she persuaded her elderly mother to sign up for the same transport, fearing to leave her behind in Theresienstadt. Her mother was working in the mica barracks at the time, thereby enjoying a degree of protection from the transports. Meanwhile Gertrude was struck from the transport list but was unable to persuade the authorities to delete her mother's name. For days they tried to hide, creeping from attic to attic, once moving six times in the course of one night. Nobody wanted to help them, for fear of being transported themselves as a penalty. After a week of living like fugitives they reported to the transport barrack and two days later arrived in Auschwitz. 'I shall never get the picture out of my mind. I see it in

6. Quoted in *Women in the Resistance and in the Holocaust*, ed. Vera Laska, p. 237.
7. Klara Caro, p. 22.
8. 'Theresienstadt von einer Blinden erlebt und niedergeschrieben', p. 4.
9. 'Erinnerungen an Theresienstadt', p. 6.

slow motion. My mother did not turn around. She left slowly and softly, through the big iron gate. She didn't turn around to look at me. Recently when I saw in "Shoah" the big gate in Birkenau, everything came back to me again.'[10] An excerpt taken from *Terezin*, published by the Council of Jewish Communities in Czech Lands, provides this grotesque detail:

> The Nazis are so sure that the prisoners are unaware of their destination, and that they still believe what they are being told, that they threaten those who do not join their transport or try to avoid it in some way with sending them to a concentration camp! People no longer go to bed because nobody can fall asleep anyway. Everything disintegrates, nobody is interested in anything, only transports loom in everybody's mind. Night changes into day, nerves are tensed to breaking point, there is only hope and despair, waiting, desperate waiting. Lodgings are empty, remnants of left-behind property lie about everywhere that nobody can be bothered with.[11]

This threat, of course, conveys the message that the Nazis wanted to transmit—the perception that Theresienstadt was benign.

The most poignant narratives are those describing individual leave-taking. Trude Groag writes about her last moments with her mother:

> Departure day had come. We were sitting in the departure area of the sluice. I urged my mother to keep on being brave and to wait for us and for the end of the war in her new abode. It had to be coming soon. She was rather quiet and we only spoke about a reunion. Suddenly there was a movement and then deathly silence. The SS arrived, the blood froze in our veins, fear paralysed those waiting. Numbers were called. My brother went first. 'If it goes badly with me', he whispered softly in my ear, 'I have had a good life and maybe I can help Mother.' Suddenly he had disappeared in the crowd. Then my mother's number was called. She walked with her head held high to the transport truck. She stood to the front when she got on. A thick, damp, cold mist enveloped everything. Another look, a wave; on the other side my brother was heading in a different direction by foot. O God! In a few seconds a world of love had been swallowed up. And those of

---

10. *Ich geb Dir einen Mantel*, ed. Berger *et al.*, p. 57.
11. *Terezin*, ed. Ehrmann, Heitlinger and Iltis, p. 39.

us who were left, miserable as we were, were already building our hope of a reunion.[12]

Morsel recalls her last sight of her brother: 'Mercifully, my father died very quickly, but not before he saw my brother, whose transport remained in Terezin only overnight. I shall forever see my brother standing in the cattle car before the door was shut. The thousand people from this transport disappeared without a trace; there was not a single survivor after the war'.[13]

In Ilse Blumenthal-Weiss's poem, 'In Memoriam', written years after the farewell from her husband, the agony of the separation has not been diminished by time. The poem is printed in German in Appendix B.

> Snowed in by final hours
> In the dark sluice of farewell.
> Our eyes were gaping wounds.
> Our words eternal sounds.
>
> Once more we gave as gifts
> All that we knew of life.
> The last look. We had to part.
> Your tears rained deep into my heart.
>
> Hands extended over me in blessing
> You prayed me for the last time.
> And now without you I go towards you
> And bear your death across a wide world.

Miriam Merzbacher-Blumenthal, a survivor of Theresienstadt, witnessed as a teenager the parting of parents from their one-year-old daughter. She later wrote about it in a poem entitled 'The Lord bless you and keep you' (printed in German below, 148–9).

> Left, right
> Right, left
> A mother knits a dress
> For her child.
> Left, right
> Right, left,
> She is knitting a blue dress.

12. 'Namen und Ortschaften in Erinnerungen der Frau Trude Groag', p. 16.
13. Quoted in *Women in the Resistance*, ed. Laska, p. 235.

Left, right
Right, left
'The Lord bless you
And keep you.
The Lord has given,'
Left, right
'The Lord has taken away,'
Right, left,
'The name of the Lord
Be praised.'

Left, right
Right, left
A girl outgrew the blue dress,
Left, right
Blessed
And guarded,
Right, left . . .
The Lord has given
The ovens have taken
Parents and brother—
Left, right
Right, left!

Left, right
Right, left
'Oh Lord, Thy name be praised!
Left, right
Right, left.
Glorified and hallowed
Praised and extolled.
Left, right
Oh Lord
The ovens!
May your name be praised,
Left, right
Right, left.

These are among the stillest of the still-life portraits of the Holocaust.

Deep friendships were often forged among women who themselves had been spared but who had lost close relatives in a transport. The rupture in turn of these friendships by a further transport meant yet another leave-taking, another devastating loss. Gerty Spies describes her loss when her friend Martha Geißmar, the violinist, left on a transport. She writes of their last moments together:

> I have rarely seen a human being part with such suffering. With tender, unabashed sadness she moved away from life and people, disappointed by both. 'You are the only one I'm grieving for,' she said several times. We parted at evening in the pitch dark street. 'Good-bye,' she said softly and kissed me.[14]

Käthe Starke, who had left her cleaning job to work in the library, writes about returning to work after the most devastating of the transports:

> After this transport our hearts were empty, the streets were empty and the sidewalks were empty. The silence of death had entered the anthills of Theresienstadt. After four weeks filled with fear, agitation, the pain of separation, a workload that had now doubled and even tripled, slowly our feeble lives re-emerged from a deep, exhausted sleep.
> On the morning of the 29th of October I opened up the library. That was now my duty. I had the feeling that I had not set foot in it since the 28th of September and that's the way it also looked. The window shades were drawn and I left them that way. Dark spaces gaped in the shelves where busy hands had been brutally interrupted. I bent down at random and started to arrange some books, just to bring some life into the stiff, uncanny loneliness of the place. There was a movement at the door. Abrahamson came in. In the dim light we looked at each other. He had clearly aged in the last four weeks. I could tell by his expression that he was thinking the same as I was. After a long illness Professor Utitz became the chief librarian again. I was promoted to be his deputy, an escalated career typical of Theresienstadt—from a counter-job to deputy librarian in eight months. Death opened up jobs. One wave of the hand brought a successor, another wave replaced him. . . . I am the fourth deputy in twenty-two months, the fourth and the last, but at this point I do not know that.[15]

The immediate effects of the transports were increased manual labour and longer work hours for women who now assumed jobs previously held by men. Dormitzer writes: 'The mass deportations

---

14. *Drei Jahre Theresienstadt*, p. 88.
15. *Der Führer schenkt den Juden eine Stadt*, p. 151.

of the autumn of 1944 robbed all offices and work places of the majority of their employees. Thus it became necessary that old people (all over sixty-five were spared deportation) had to take their places. I started work in October 1944 in the post office and kept my job until the liberation.'[16]

The following two excerpts expose the reality of what awaited the transports once they arrived in Auschwitz. The twins Ruth and Eva Herskowitz, teenagers at the time, were among those selected for a transport. As twins they were subjected to the notorious medical experiments of Dr Mengele. Both survived but Ruth spent months recuperating in a Swedish hospital. In this excerpt from a letter written to the Caro family, presumably that of Klara Caro whose memoirs are often quoted in this book, Eva gives us a chilling glimpse of the 'family camp' of Birkenau, a satellite camp of Auschwitz.

> Ruth and I went along with the other twins to the big women's camp. On the 10th of July Father went with 8000 others to a martyr's death. That night I stood outside and looked at the closed trucks driving to and from the crematorium. I knew that Daddy was sitting in one of these trucks and was thinking of us for the last time. The fire was burning in the chimney and it smelled, as always in Birkenau, of bones. Yet that night did indeed end, and despite all the cruelty we did not lose our sanity. Nor did we behave like those in despair. No, our horror was so enormous that we became apathetic.
>
> All of Theresienstadt arrived in October. I personally witnessed many of my friends walking past me right into the gas chambers, but my hands were tied and I could not help them.[17]

The fate of yet another Theresienstadt transport, described in Vera Laska's 'Auschwitz—a Factual Deposition', gives Holocaust literature a powerful memory of defiant courage demonstrated by a group of Czech Jews moments before their death.

> To prevent resistance, entire blocks were told that volunteers were needed for factory work in Germany. Most of the volunteers ended up in the gas chambers. So did the Czech transport from Terezin that had been kept alive for half a year in the exceptional family blocks. The SS used them for propaganda, or just loved to

16. 'Erlebnisse in Nürnberg', pp. 4–5.
17. Eva Herskowitz, p. 3.

play cat and mouse games. These unfortunate people were packed off on Masaryk's birthday, March 7, and were told that they were being moved to another work camp. The following night they were all gassed. They entered the gas chambers singing the national anthem. Their postcards, an especially cruel Nazi custom, were postdated March 25, and arrived at Terezin postmarked from Dachau, stating that all was well. This was supposed to keep further transports from Terezin calm.

In another Terezin group the women had a chance to be sent to work camps in the Reich. But mothers would not leave their children and in July 1944 accompanied them into the gas. One of the 15,000 children in Terezin had written in a poem, 'I never saw another butterfly'. Few ever did. Barely one hundred of them survived.[18]

Blumenthal-Weiss's poem 'Departure of the Transport' is a heart-breaking enlargement of a transport photo.

> I have seen children, sick and wasted with fever.
> They were so quiet. Did not lift a finger.
> They shoved them into a dark,
> Dirty old cattle car
> And left them all on their own. . . .
> Wee children . . . left all on their own.
>
> I have seen women, sick and faceless.
> They were so quiet. They did not stir.
> They shoved them into a dark,
> Dirty old cattle car.
> There they lay
> In fear and horror,
> Those ill women.
>
> I have seen men, reduced to a heap.
> They were all centuries old.
> They shoved them into a dark,
> Dirty cattle car for transport.—
> Now keep on going,
> Keep on rolling up the tracks
> To torture and extinction.[19]

18. Quoted in *Women in the Resistance*, ed. Laska, p. 182.
19. *Mahnmal*, p. 25. The poem is printed in German in Appendix B.

The status of Theresienstadt was meanwhile being discussed at the highest level of command, the central issue being whether to reorganize it as an extermination camp, which would mean building gas chambers, or maintain its image as a Jewish resettlement oasis. Memoirs show that rumours of the former were rampant. Sternberg, for example, writes, 'At the same time we had to build gas chambers in Theresienstadt because it was feared that Auschwitz would probably no longer be able to manage the last large transport.'[20] Spies has this to say:

> Each day we saw the power of our oppressors becoming weaker. It gave us all the more reason to fear that they could destroy us. Windowless barracks facing toward the outside were being built in a circle on the bulwarks. . . . Like a phantom the word 'gassing' would be passed at times from mouth to mouth. We had heard talk about it but nobody knew for sure. Much later we found out that gas had been delivered and that we had been miraculously saved at the last minute by the Red Cross. But an undefined fear dogged our footsteps and never left us for an hour.[21]

Another memoir shows how much this new anxiety oppressed them.

> The ghetto was to be replenished, so the rumour went. We were driven to work. New barracks were built, much to our astonishment. Wasn't there enough space in spite of the new arrivals? Had not Theresienstadt housed 60,000 people and now there were hardly 19,000? Why these remote barracks on the bastion which had such a strange appearance? It struck us as strange that they had no windows. Were we supposed to live in them? . . .
>
> Only after the collapse did it become known that these strange structures were to serve as gas chambers.[22]

Although records do not agree exactly as to when it happened, there is no doubt that the disposal of urns did happen during the final months of the camp. Along with the census, it was as gruesome a single event as happened in the course of the inmates' entire internment. Its onslaught on the sensibilities of the women can be gathered from the following excerpts. Groag describes it like this:

---

20. Alexandra Sternberg, p. 5.
21. *Drei Jahre Theresienstadt*, p. 88.
22. Edith Kramer, 'Hell and Rebirth', pp. 18–19.

What was this black mass of people standing on both sides of the open gate? And what about the truck they were loading with boxes? As I approached I saw something terrible. In the middle of the gate stood Murmelstein the chief Jewish Elder giving orders, his face distorted with grief.

Long chains of people stood shoulder to shoulder, women, children and old people handing the urns of our dead to one another, just like masons passing bricks on a building site. . . .

Opposite on a bridge an SS man was casually leaning, observing the spectacle.

My heart stopped and I could scarcely go on. Then I heard a little boy whispering words of comfort in rude Theresienstadt jargon: 'Don't cry, Mother, if I come upon Grandmother I'll steal from her.'[23]

The simile of bricks is particularly painful when one considers that in Christian theology believers are compared to 'living stones', collectively forming a living organism—the Church. In this context Jews have been reduced to dead bricks extracted from a building and conveyed to a river. Eisenkraft writes:

You can imagine how upsetting the work was. Many who had lost loved ones were hoping for a reunion, at least with their remains. . . . In this way I heard the woman next to me suddenly cry out: 'My husband, my husband!' Because the work was not allowed to stop I pushed her out of the row to prevent the supervisor from becoming suspicious; the women on the left and right then filled the gap. She was not sure, however, what to do with her find and how to conceal it. She therefore tried simply to disappear, with the thought of carrying the urn back to her lodgings, packing it among her belongings, to be taken later to her home country. But one of the Jewish supervisors noticed her and brought her back into the line again with bitter reproaches.[24]

Jacob Presser tells a macabre anecdote about the disposal of the urns showing how appallingly low the value of a human life had sunk:

When the writer [i.e. Presser] looked the place over in 1958, on a still September evening, after travelling some forty miles from

23. 'Namen und Ortschaften', pp. 20–1.
24. *Damals in Theresienstadt*, p. 70.

Prague, his main impression was one of a ghost town—where once so many thousands had been crammed together, hardly a soul was now to be seen. There was no sound at all, not even on the large central square. The writer went to the barracks, the crematorium, the fort, taking everything in, and listening to his two guides, who had been there as children.

One of them told how he was allowed to help clear the 'mausoleum', the cellar where the ashes of the dead were stored. These ashes were to be thrown into the river Eger, and for this work volunteers were given a tin of sardines apiece. 'We had a rare old time and on top of it—sardines. . . .' The ashes were kept in three types of boxes, all with a label bearing the name, birth-date and date of death; prominent camp inmates had iron boxes, the less distinguished had wooden boxes, and the rest cardboard ones. The mausoleum was cleared a hundred boxes at a time. We would toss them to one another and, in the case of iron, yell out, 'Look out, here comes another celebrity.' Quite often a tooth or something would fall out, which we would throw into another box. The best fun of all was mixing together the big shots and the lesser lights.

A number of adults were present at the Eger as well: one eye-witness says that, between them, they disposed not of 30,000 but of 40,000 boxes: 'The whole thing was like a ball game, with the boxes being tossed from hand to hand.' One of the witnesses, however, felt that she simply could not continue, not even for the extra sardines. When she complained, the Germans allowed her to stop; an old lady was let off as well, but a third woman, who complained of a weak heart, was refused: 'If I let you off, everyone's going to have heart trouble.'[25]

Death was thus being handled as a ball game with women and children being used to keep the game going. One anonymous report may have been written by the woman described above who refused to take part; after stating her refusal she adds: 'For four days women, men and children dug up numbered boxes from the urn-graveyard. I do not know what they did with them. Could these ashes have been used as a fertilizer? I am not an expert in agricultural matters.'[26]

The emptying of the cells within the fortress walls (casemates) had, though, even more practical and sinister motives than the disposal of human remains.

25. Jacob Presser- *The Destruction of the Dutch Jews*, p. 531.
26. 'Der Tod in Theresienstadt', p. 7.

One day, shortly before the end of the war, I was ordered to these casemates to be part of a human chain stretching to the river. We were removing the urns with the ashes, passing them from hand to hand, to be finally thrown into the river. For days upon end there were ashes floating on the surface. We all thought that the Nazis wanted to destroy the evidence, but actually they were emptying the casemates to turn them into gas chambers. The windows of the casemates were cemented, and there was a railroad car stationed close by. We found out later that it contained canisters of poisonous gas pellets. The camp commandant, Karl Rahm, reported this to the International Red Cross in Geneva. That saved our lives, as well as his.[27]

Transport anxiety had become so ingrained in their psyche that when the inmates were offered the opportunity in February 1945 to leave on a transport to a neutral country—Switzerland—the offer was met with distrust, scepticism, and by many with flat rejection. The women who opted to go, judging from the memoirs recording the incident, encapsulate the emotional history of Theresienstadt— anxiety, hope, fear, renewed anxiety as they approach the border, paranoia when the train unexpectedly stops, the elation of being free, and finally coping with survival. Postcards soon arrived in Theresienstadt, with the assurance that the transport was not a hoax. Caro's journal provides details of the journey.

Our journey led us past ruined Nürnberg, past the remains of burnt-out trains, past the ruins of Ulm and Friedrichshafen. A man in civilian dress and without a badge suddenly appeared in the train and said: 'In the name of the Führer you may now remove your star.' It is hard to describe this historic moment, when even the doubters among us began to believe. And so we took off the sign that had been designed to humiliate and dishon- our us, that we had nevertheless worn with our heads high, proud of our Jewishness. Outside Constance we stopped for the whole night on a very dark stretch. Nobody knew what it meant and once more many began to panic. But the next morning we continued on our way. The order was given for men to tidy themselves up and for women to brush their hair. Then we saw for the last time in the German railway station in Constance the insignia of tyranny, repression and darkness and we proceeded into God's garden, into glorious Switzerland, into the freedom we

27. Quoted in *Women in the Resistance*, ed. Laska, p. 235.

longed for so intensely. Words cannot describe what we felt when friendly people, waving in welcome, received us and Red Cross nurses handed us delicacies which we no longer knew—apples, cigarettes and chocolate. But the first thing we did when the train was on Swiss ground was to say *Kaddisch* for loved ones, who were not experiencing this hour of liberation, this *Jezias Mizrajim* [exodus from Egypt].[28]

Edith Kramer's account of the journey to Switzerland alludes to the same anxiety that is described by Klara Caro, lacks the overt expression of Caro's piety but contains some humorous touches, that are lacking in Klara Caro's memoir.

Towards the end of the war, in February 1945, I was liberated from Theresienstadt concentration camp and sent to Switzerland. A rumour persisted that the transport to Switzerland had been arranged by the Red Cross, but this was not the case. We learned later that at the time Germany was in urgent need of iron ore from Sweden and could not get it because Sweden asked for payment in gold. Consequently, Himmler, who wanted to save his hide in case of defeat, entered into negotiations with a very high former official of the Swiss Government, Alt-Bundesrat Mussy, and offered the release of Jews against payment in gold. It had been known that American Jews were willing to pay for the release of their relatives, ever since they had heard that concentration camps existed.

Early in 1945 the deal came off but, as most of the nominated relatives of Americans had already been murdered, their place on the transport was taken by others (mainly of the Nazis own choosing). . . .

Finally on the third day we approached the Swiss frontier. We were told by the SS men to take off the Stars of David ('Judensterne') and to beautify. They even distributed lipsticks for this purpose. This was the last order the SS issued and this they admitted. They withdrew and wished us—to our enormous astonishment—all the best. Only now did we realize that we were really going towards freedom. Married couples embraced, many wept and sobbed. It was unbelievable that we should be free. Only youth was not quite so sentimental, a young girl sang when the Gestapo went: 'Say softly servus as farewell' and 'Who will weep when we separate. . .'.

28. Klara Caro, p. 25.

But once again our confidence was shaken. Shortly before the Swiss frontier the train stopped for hours in front of a barn. Many doubted that we would be allowed into Switzerland. The Gestapo would lead us into this large barn and kill us there. The whole night was spent in terrible suspense but next morning the train rolled slowly into Kreuzlingen station.

It was pointed out to us that reporters would interview us about our experiences in Theresienstadt. In view of later transports we shouldn't say anything unfavourable. When the reporters finally came we followed these instructions. Only an old granny, who was deaf and had heard nothing, told freely—the reporters shouted the questions into her ears—how much she had suffered and described the terrible conditions. All this appeared promptly in the newspapers.[29]

The following quotation from a later account adds an interesting political perspective to the successful Swiss transport.

After Hitler heard that on 6 February 1945 Himmler had allowed twelve hundred Jews coming from Theresienstadt to enter Switzerland—the news was published in two Swiss papers on 8 February—he made such a violent scene in front of the RFSS that Himmler again revoked all relief measures for the Jews and instructed Hermann Pister, the commander of the Buchenwald concentration camp, not to allow any concentration camp prisoners in southern Germany to pass into enemy hands alive.[30]

Another pleasant reminder of the existence of a safe, welcoming world happened on 13 April 1945 when the entire Danish contingent left in comfortable coaches provided by Sweden. Their departure, amid much fanfare and music, gave Theresienstadt its only unambiguous celebration. People swarmed around the large comfortable coaches; several writers comment that the Swedish drivers refused to allow the SS men to have a closer look at the luxurious interiors.

The final six months of the camp oscillated between catastrophe and celebration. The Swiss transport had hardly left when mass transports started arriving in Theresienstadt, bringing with them the full implications of the transports to the East. Any residual illusion of Birkenau as a family collapse. Dormitzer tells us what happened:

29. Kramer, 'Hell and Rebirth', pp. 6 and 23–5.
30. Gerald Fleming, *Hitler and the Final Solution*, p. 170.

In March 1945 to our general amazement transports came back again to Theresienstadt from very different camps in Poland and Germany; indeed in an indescribable condition, staggering through the streets like living corpses, for the most part so weak that the majority of them died. A whole freight-car full of corpses also arrived, and in the shower-room of the main bathhouse where these people were to be washed, twenty-five people dropped dead from weakness when the hot water touched them. None of them looked human any more; they looked more like wild animals.[31]

These transports continued to arrive virtually until the camp was liberated in May. The descriptions given of them defy comment and are among the hardest to read of all the memoirs. Lederer takes up the story:

A few—so very few—were now back in Theresienstadt, and with them had come others who had never been in the ghetto. They were being taken from the trucks, some of them writhing in convulsions, and bedded on the grass. There they sat or lay, thousands of emaciated Jobs—'My bone cleaveth to my skin and to my flesh'. Young though they were, they looked aged. They were too weak to walk or even to move. They were swarming with lice, covered with ulcers ad running sores—'my flesh is clothed with worms and clods of dust; my skin is broken and become loathsome'. They wore thin rags that they had taken off corpses that still lay in the trucks—'they cause the naked to lodge without clothing, that they have no covering in the cold'. The eyes of many were clouded by the enormity of suffering that had passed the farthest limits of endurance: they were apathetic and indifferent to their fate. The eyes of others were shining with a feverish brilliance, they greedily swallowed every scrap of food, and, their whole body trembling, they spoke of their fellow-sufferers.

But not all of them had come by train. Many had walked hundreds of miles.[32]

One of those returning by foot was Grete Salus, who had been transported along with her physician husband in October from Theresienstadt, survived both Auschwitz and Oderan and was now returning 'home' to Theresienstadt, having lost her husband in Auschwitz. It was Saturday 21 April.

31. 'Leben in Theresienstadt', p. 5.
32. *Ghetto Theresienstadt*, p. 188.

We staggered through a cordon of people. It had become deathly silent. People held hands to protect us from the crowd that was descending upon us. Yet even with this the human chain was broken when a mother saw her daughter. Dear God, I cannot begin to describe what happened to us that day, for its brutal force almost tore us apart. We had, after all, been presumed as good as dead and now had returned safely to the ghetto, the first of the larger transports of women from Theresienstadt.[33]

Although cultural activities were no longer officially promoted, the few remaining artists who had miraculously escaped the October transports made some half-hearted attempts to perform for one another, but after the first transport from the East, these too stopped. Ulrike Migdal cites the response of the singer, Hedda Grab: 'Now we knew the truth, and from that day on all singing, plays, all distractions stopped. None of us could bring ourselves to sing any more.'[34]

An epidemic of typhus, carried by victims of the transports, spread quickly but was vigorously combated by a team of doctors and nurses, united in a joint effort that contrasts sharply with previous fragmented relationships between the various groups. This is how Jacobsohn describes it in 'The Daily Life':

One infected another, so that spotted fever, typhoid, dysentery, etc., became rampant. So many died that it became impossible to bury or cremate all of them. The stench of the corpses spread all over the barracks and the town. We feared that not one of the inhabitants of Theresienstadt would see his home again.

But, tirelessly, the Russians brought food and medicaments. One lorry after another arrived with flour, etc. on the very evening of the liberation. The Russian Commander called all the heads of the houses, barracks and offices together and declared that the Russians had come to liberate the Jews. A miracle had happened. Although many measures were taken at once to remedy the untenable, almost incredible state of affairs, some weeks went by before a real improvement was noticeable. Strong measures were adopted to remove the filth which had collected throughout the years. In the so-called Hamburg Barracks you could wade up to the knees in dirt. In the Bodenbach barracks the sick lay on the bare floor, crammed together, and spread their diseases.[35]

33. *Eine Frau erzählt*, p. 85.
34. *Und die Musik spielt dazu*, p. 55.
35. 'The Daily Life', p. 19.

External forces were now shaping the destiny of Theresienstadt, foretelling the end of its time as a concentration camp. Breslauer writes: 'From the windows we could watch air attacks on nearby Leitmeritz and we followed the course of events with the greatest interest.'[36] Memoirs tell of a haze of smoke lying for days over the whole town, the result of the daily incineration of camp records. Oestreicher, who was in charge of the kitchens, says that the SS had biscuits baked for them in preparation for flight—a claim that Sternberg confirms: 'We noticed a tremendous nervousness about the SS. The order was given to bake more bread. We found out from the orderlies (Jewish men who had to wait on SS people) that the SS were providing themselves in a striking way with food items and that they had civilian clothes at the ready.'[37]

Memoirs dealing with the unfurling of these events reveal a different tone and betray new anxieties and vulnerabilities. Spies's account is touched with an elegaic quality as she recaptures the memory of liberation when it came at last on 8 May 1945.

> There were lovely, hot summer days. In the evening when everything was quiet you could hear the Russians singing their sad songs in their camp in the open air.
>
> I found a job in the dietary kitchen, had finally enough to eat and got sick from over-eating. . . . After recuperating I worked in the pharmacy where I felt happy and at home. My boss Anna Horpazka was from Prague. She was a slender, pretty blonde woman and ran around in trousers . . . hands in her pockets and smoked, which was lavishly permitted since the arrival of the Russians. . . .
>
> We were now allowed to go up on the ramparts during our lunch break. I would lie up there, listen to the trees rustle and watch the clouds—freedom! Were we really free?. . .[38]

Morsel did not know she was free until the Russians came: 'We were liberated by the Russian army in early May 1945. All the SS men had disappeared during the night, yet we had no idea that we were free until the Russians arrived.'[39]

Dormitzer celebrates the liberation in verse:

36. 'Erinnerungen an Theresienstadt', p. 11.
37. Alexandra Sternberg, p. 5.
38. *Drei Jahre Theresienstadt*, p. 91.
39. *Women in the Resistance*, ed. Laska, p. 237.

Finale

A day like all the others, desolate and empty.
In our minds not a ray of hope;
The clock set at the same redundant time,
Punctuated only by the same poor rations.
Deeply dejected we go to bed
And close exhausted eyes.
Next morning the miracle has come about:
Foreign uniforms mill about,
Russians redeeming us from slavery.
We hear laughing, weeping, rejoicing, screaming.
We rub our eyes—it's a fancy dream
That will burst soon like a soap bubble.
No, they're there. The Spectre is gone.
Hurrah, Hosanna; we can go home,
We are at the start of beastless days.
To You, Unredundant One, we hoist joyful sail
We give You bliss back and our souls' tale,
You have rescued Your people Israel![40]

Breslauer's brief comments are also a reminder that the beautification programme was a thing of the past. After the Russians came in on 8 May German street signs were replaced with Czech ones. She notes the following irony: 'Russians' horses were now grazing on the well-manicured lawns of the town, which soon could not be recognized.'[41]

Sternberg's memoir of the liberation provides the startling anecdote about old Mr Falkenstein who survived the camp by unwittingly defeating the Nazis at their favourite game—keeping records.

The food improved considerably. I took on nursing duties and because of this was one of the last to return to Germany. Dr Fabian was in the same returning transport, as well as Mr Falkenstein, who was over a hundred years of age. Herr Falkenstein owes his survival to a fluke of German bureaucracy. There were summons, for example, that ordered all people between seventy and eighty years of age to get ready for a transport to Auschwitz. But it never occurred to anybody that there was a hundred-year-old among us. This circumstance allowed Mr Falkenstein to live, and his daughter is today employed in the Jewish

40. *Theresienstädter Bilder*, p. 21. The poem is printed in German in Appendix A.
41. 'Erinnerungen an Theresienstadt', p. 11.

hospital in Berlin.[42]

The task of repatriation was enormous, and was hampered by the total collapse of Germany's infrastructure. Buses were sent from all the major cities to bring people 'home'. Many were fetched by relatives and driven away by car. 'It was not easy', writes Breslauer, 'to say goodbye to the people who had shared the sufferings of these years and despite our joy, many a tear was shed.'[43] Spies's farewell from her Czech friend has no hint of the finality of a friendship, that a new political reality would soon break.

The farewell [from Anna Horpazka] was brief: 'Frau Spies, you know that I have become very fond of you. Do write.' I wrote to her several times but never received a reply. My letters must have got stuck in the censor between nations who would like to love one another. Finally I gave up because I did not want her to get into trouble. What has become of Anna Horpazka?[44]

Just as the Jews' arrival in Theresienstadt had been heralded by symbols of death, so their liberation was organized in the presence of emaciated skeletons who roamed the streets. The following impressions were recorded by a Jewish American soldier:

A terrible street is the Bahnhofstrasse, where the trains pull in right into the street, either to discharge those poor victims or to take them away with destination unknown. I happened to see a train that had just returned from Hungary and had brought back the first transport of Jews to their home towns. The train was just being cleaned and the whole street was full of the garbage and the stench was almost unbearable. We walked through the town and people explained to us all the different functions of this house and that barrack and this cave, etc., and it was just a horrible sight. People move around the place, little kids, young boys and girls and old people. They all live under a 'camp' influence and to them things look different. They tell you 'my mother was gassed' or 'my husband was killed in Buchenwald' as every normal person would refer to 'I saw a nice movie last night'. One told me at times they had to walk up the stairs very slowly, otherwise they would have lost excessive weight and that they couldn't afford with the poor

42. Alexandra Sternberg, p. 5. The particulars of each individual were entered in no fewer than twelve different index cards. Lederer, *Ghetto Theresienstadt*, p. 57.

43. 'Erinnerungen an Theresienstadt', p. 11.

44. *Drei Jahre Theresienstadt*, p. 93.

and insufficient meals they got. I saw skeletons walking around on sticks, to keep themselves up, victims of concentration camps, who just had gotten there, pale like a white sheet of paper, their eyes without any expression, moving around, apparently for no reason at all; some talking to themselves.[45]

Lederer points out that most doctors and nurses opted to stay after the liberation and help fight the typhus epidemic.

Words cannot convey their selfless courage and devotion, nor mourn the tragedy of those among them who having contracted the disease while doing their work of charity died without having enjoyed their release from bondage. . . . Altogether 502 of the former prisoners succumbed to the disease in the period from April 21 to June 30, 1945; the overall mortality rate was 22.9 per cent. Among those former prisoners of the ghetto who had contracted typhus, the mortality rate was 38 per cent; among these victims were eighty who had contracted the disease while assisting their suffering fellow-prisoners. Those who thus gave their lives included fifteen doctors, fifteen nurses and thirteen orderlies from the delousing station.[46]

One of these nurses was Mina Wolfenstein, who has left us several poems about her internment in Theresienstadt.

The awful task of locating missing relatives had begun. For some, like Trude Groag, it was a fruitful search. She had asked permission to go to Prague to find her son. Her memoir describes their meeting but provides no explanation of her son's military involvement.

I asked a group of soldiers if they happened to know anything about a Hans Groag. No, maybe he's with the African Corps. So where do I go now? Then a sun-burned fellow comes by. I repeat the question. But, of course, he's standing over there beside the third jeep. Don't you recognize me? I am Teitelbaum from Troppau. I barely hear what he is saying. I am already running towards the third jeep, on which Hans is busy fixing something. What a moment! What happiness! Both of us are ecstatic. Where to begin? Hans takes a cushion from the jeep, sets me down under a tree, brings warm water from the jeep and a dazzling white handkerchief. Ah God! What joy![47]

45. Eric Lipman, 'A Trip to Ghetto Theresienstadt', p. 3.
46. *Ghetto Theresienstadt*, pp. 192–5.
47. 'Namen und Ortschaften', p. 26.

Dormitzer's account of the initial steps of repatriation, by contrast, recalls the antagonism between the two groups returning to Holland, and in fact describes her departure from Theresienstadt in much the same terms as her arrival. The one major difference, which she does not note, is that she had meanwhile become a widow.

After the end of the war former prisoners were grouped together according to the country of origin of their transport, which also was the case for the officials of the self-government. We emigrants who had lived in Holland were counted with the Dutch contingent, but the Dutch Jews behaved in a very unfriendly way to the emigrants who were almost all able to speak Dutch. They accused them of being 'guilty of the plight of Dutch Jews'. This hostility was not just confined to inmates but was also practised by responsible Dutch officials. It was even felt when the Dutch group was registering for the transport home. First the native Dutch were taken, then after waiting nervously for an hour it was the emigrants' turn. The whole group was made up of about 1650 people.

On the 7th of June 1945 the group was called to be in the courtyard of Barracks BV at half past seven in the morning. All Dutch people were to leave in a transport, and now the lists were checked. Because of lack of space each person was only allowed to take one case. Those who owned more entrusted their things to friends from Prague, to be forwarded later. Everybody leaving Theresienstadt could claim 1000 Czech crowns which was paid out by the former camp bank and was considered compensation for the compulsory balance of ghetto money. I didn't get anything because the bank didn't have any money then. We had to wait many hours in the barrack's courtyard and got one meal. Finally we were supposed to go to the Little Fortress with its evil reputation for many executions; we had to walk part of the way which meant that we all had to carry our own baggage. Open trucks provided our transport for the rest of the way. In the Little Fortress we were disinfected with DDT by French RK-nurses. Then each person was called individually by name. There was real confusion, the Dutch-Jewish transport doctor behaved badly, and finally we left the Little Fortress and Theresienstadt at five o'clock in the afternoon on large French Kommando trucks. They were overcrowded beyond description; we had to sit on our cases and were hungry.[48]

48. Dormitzer, 'Erlebnisse in Nürnberg', p. 5.

Eisenkraft celebrates her new freedom with unrestrained joy.

> I had survived all my illnesses and deliberate humiliation without permanent physical and emotional damage and now I was actually on my way home. . . . What a joyful feeling! Free of fear and hunger and vermin and tortures. What a glorious feeling! To be free again after one and a half years, actually after twelve years. Not to be a sub-human, defamed, oppressed, guarded, fettered, but a free person like other people.[49]

Eisenkraft's experience of liberation is in total contrast to the self-portrait drawn by Salus of a woman stumbling through the streets of Prague half-crazed by grief. In her desire to go home she had opted to defy the quarantine ruling and leave Theresienstadt without permission. She describes her return home:

> One morning I succeeded in slipping away. For part of the way I got a ride on a Russian armoured car. Every time we talked in Theresienstadt about liberation we always used to say: 'I want to walk the whole way back to Prague.' I too wanted to do that. I covered the second half of the journey to freedom and to Prague by foot. Not celebrating and jubilating, as I used to imagine, but filled with dread and fear. Prague—I walked through the streets in amazement. There was indeed still a city in which one could walk alone. People were walking about casually, not realizing what a miracle it was to be able to do that. I sensed that people were looking at me, that every gaze was fixed on me. People were indeed looking at me, for suddenly I felt a little parcel in my hand. When I opened it, it was filled with sweets. A kind gesture extended by some kind hand. Then I realized that I was absolutely on my own. My husband—I kept looking for my husband. Slowly streets were changing to voices. Voices of the past now chased me mercilessly from one grave to another.
>
> A woman said to me: 'Why such despair, everything is going to be fine.' A human voice was speaking to me in my awful aloneness. Tears poured down my face. Sobbing, I kept wandering around aimlessly and I couldn't stop crying. My husband was gone—my parents—millions were gone—at the wave of a wicked, murderer's hand.[50]

49. *Damals in Theresienstadt*, p. 99.
50. *Eine Frau erzählt*, p. 99.

Dormitzer's account of the journey back to Holland is a detailed travel documentary of war-ravaged Germany, a shocking picture of devastation and destruction.

We drove through towns that were in ruins and passed Karlsbad. We spent the night in a castle in West Bohemia. After a prolonged stay there we finally left on the 11th of June by car, still not crossing the German border that day but were lodged in a cinema on straw bedding in another place in Bohemia. We had to spend a full week there. The Sudeten-German population behaved in a very hostile way towards us. We once had a service conducted by a Rabbi from the American Army. Our journey was continued on the 18th using English buses. We drove through Frankish Switzerland and I knew that now we had to be approaching Nürnberg but I did not recognize the ruined city that we drove through; I was not able to speak as we drove through. The buses took us as far as Bamberg where we had a hard time finding accommodation. On the next day, the 19th, we were loaded into cattle cars. At night they were locked and stayed unlighted. No provision had been made in them for physical necessities. Washrooms in railway stations could not be used; there were warnings posted everywhere about the danger of typhus. Our journey took us through Frankfurt, then we came to the Rhine, where the train had to wait many hours because of the heavy rail traffic that was being directed over a temporary bridge. We travelled along the left bank of the Rhine as far as Bonn from where the train proceeded to Maastricht by way of Aachen, in order to avoid Cologne.

We arrived on the 21st of June and except for lukewarm milk did not get anything to eat, but even worse was the fact that we were not released as anticipated but were taken to a quarantine camp in Sittard. They registered us during the night there. Most were then taken to Lynbroek monastery which was located near there. The Dutch were soon released while the emigrants remained interned, guarded by Dutch soldiers with guns. The food, delivered to us by Americans, was good. My sister had a serious eye problem and was supposed to consult an opthalmologist. Permission was given with difficulty and my sister was escorted there and back by an armed soldier. One Sunday my daughter came from Hilversum with my son-in-law to procure my release. She was denied her request by an unfriendly Dutch C.O. The same thing was repeated the following Sunday. It was only after a protest was sent to England that we were granted freedom of movement. On the 11th of July 1945 at nine o'clock in the evening my sister and I left the monastery in a rented car, paid for by my children at great personal sacrifice. Our journey took us over vast stretches of roads that were still destroyed all the way to Hilversum, where we arrived the next day at three in the morning. Many of my former Theresienstadt companions in suffering remained behind in Lynbroek until they found means of transport to take them to their former homes.[51]

The uncharacteristically sarcastic note she permits herself to use in her concluding sentence betrays the pain and sense of loss of a woman whose writings manifest a singular nobility of spirit: 'This period of internment in Holland was the dignified conclusion to Theresienstadt's years of suffering.' In this poem she expresses the impossibility of ever finding again what she had lost during the years of trials and internment:

Lost Years

Who'll give us back the lost years of mothers,
In which our souls were timid preachers.
We left our hot hearts after you, loved creatures,
Where are you, parents, children, sisters, brothers?

You who breathed within us in intense like-mind
Till a hard fate hit us head-on,
Destroying utterly our sing-a-long,
And took us captive to gangster minds.

Where do we begin to burrow for you all,
Nothing from your hands was given us to read.
Anxiously we query, 'Do you still breathe?'
There's nothing but streaking tears in our crawl.

What still pours hope into our ways?
The hope, Lord God, for our release.
Help your miserable ones who have no peace
And lead us back to brighter prayer-days.[52]

For some, such as Hedwig Ems, the pain of returning home, of coming back without loved ones, defies description:

---

51. 'Erlebnisse in Nürnberg', pp. 6–7.
52. *Theresienstädter Bilder*, p. 7.

I am not going to write about Berlin, bombed to pieces and totally changed, and for me now devoid of relatives and friends. It was impossible to recognize it and I would perhaps be glad to be able to leave it. I am, therefore, concluding my report about the saddest years of my life. There is still a lot I could tell but because everything I am telling is less interesting for other people, probably just like this information will be, which does not contain a single interesting event. I want to conclude, for I am not able to express my grief and pain any more for those who did not come back.[53]

Though clearly affected by her suffering, Eva Herskowitz reveals a hint of the natural resilience of youth in the aforementioned letter (p. 96) written from a refugee camp in Sweden to the Caro family: 'I want to look for light work, just like the other young girls here. It is better to work, for then you don't have time to think. I also want to earn some money for until now we were only given one coat, a dress, a pair of shoes and a set of underwear.'[54] This is a particularly touching wish in view of the suffering and humiliation she had experienced in Auschwitz.

She adds a question that is obviously not a casual enquiry, but one posed by many a camp survivor: 'Have you heard anything from mother? I don't think she is in Sweden but with the Russians. How I hope that she is alive.'[55]

Kramer's response to liberation is on some level true for all of the women. There are new anxieties, unexpected vulnerabilities along with their new freedom.

All these years we had waited for the moment of liberation and thought that now all our worries would be over. But hardly had the first excitement passed than it appeared that the energy used so far for self-preservation would be necessary for a new struggle. . . . Many felt not up to the new struggle, and even amongst my four room-mates two committed suicide, also victims of the Nazi regime. . . . Others gained strength from past experience, a strength they had never been able to foresee. They continued the battle for existence.[56]

---

53. Hedwig Ems, p. 27.
54. Eva Herskowitz, p. 5.
55. Ibid.
56. 'Hell and Rebirth', p. 25.

5

The Final Chapter

The post-Theresienstadt battle for existence is another story and it appears to be a harder one to tell than the battle for survival. As noted earlier, most of the writings are concerned with the Theresienstadt ordeal alone and end either at the camp gate or in the ruins of Germany.

At least two of the women who survived Theresienstadt—Spies and Starke—opted to stay in Germany. After several attempts to trace Dormitzer I was informed by the Netherlands State Institute for War Documentation that she had lived for some time after the war in Hilversum and that in the mid '50s she was living in London. They were unable to provide any further information about her whereabouts. Spies talks about her decision to stay in Germany with candour and forthrightness:

> I love the language in which I can and could write my poems. But above all these rich friendships give me the strength to keep me in this country. I do not only want to write letters, I want to see my friends, meet them, love them—here in this country, whose language I can speak with them. For that alone I would have stayed, if other factors too had not kept me here.[1]

She concludes: 'Germany is my home.' She also informs us that her daughter decided to emigrate to the United States with her own five-year-old daughter and died, according to Spies, of homesickness, which the doctors had not diagnosed.

Ernestine Luze returned to Vienna and shortly afterwards fell ill with tuberculosis. She spent two years in a sanatorium.

> I soon began to realize that everything had remained exactly the way it always had been. It occurred to me then that anti-semitism is still the same as it always was. I now think it will always be that way. Yes, I have to admit that I have become misanthropic. I have noticed that while standing in the tram I eavesdrop on conversations and listen for the word 'Jew' or something about

1. *Drei Jahre Theresienstadt*, pp. 15–16.

Nazis. As a Jew, of course, one is very sensitive.

In 1969 she fell into a deep depression which she first describes as descending upon her without warning but then quickly corrects herself, 'No, the experiences were already there. . . . I always was thinking about Theresienstadt.' She takes twelve pills a day and sleeps at the most three hours at night. Music is a painful reminder of the camp.

> To this day I can't bear to hear music. Only Mozart. I sometimes listen to the Requiem. Then I cry for five hours. . . . There is no way around it, one simply cannot dismiss it. One can try to level it to some extent. It doesn't have to be so brutal but it is still there.[2]

Groag and Salus both chose to emigrate to Israel where Salus's brother, her only surviving relative, was living. Salus writes:

> At that time I was living all on my own in Prague on the sixth floor of a house. I would often stand on the balcony of my room and look out. My friends and relatives were all gone and my only surviving relative was a brother in Israel. Writing helped me. The manuscript remained lying in a drawer. When I emigrated to Israel I took it with me.[3]

Kramer emigrated to Australia where she married again and practised medicine. Blumenthal-Weiss emigrated to the USA with her daughter Miriam and lived in the New York City area until her death in 1987. Morsel returned to Prague and, unlike many other deportees, was able to move into her old apartment. All she brought with her was the Yellow Star of David. She writes: 'In spite of the general rejoicing over the end of the war, I felt as if I was living in a cemetery.'[4] After a seven-year separation from her husband she was reunited with him in San Domingo. Her memoir concludes with gratitude towards San Domingo and with the reminder that the Holocaust could happen again:

> I will always remember the Dominican Republic with gratitude. We had a good life there. I heard that at the Evian conference for refugees it was the only country in the world willing to take in as many as 100,000 Jews. Unfortunately, in most cases like mine,

2. *Ich geb Dir einen Mantel*, ed. Berger *et al.*, p. 68.
3. *Eine Frau erzählt*, p. 5.
4. Quoted in *Women in the Resistance*, ed. Laska, p. 238.

those in need of a refuge could not take advantage of this generosity; the Jewish organizations were unable to get the Jews out.

I had some good years after I joined my husband. Now with three grandchildren we again have a little family. The darkness of the Holocaust did not vanish and it casts its shadow over happiness. The memories remain, and I wish them to remain.

The Yellow Star of David hangs framed in my home to commemorate six million Jews murdered for being Jewish. I do not need a reminder of the Holocaust, I have my memories. But it should be a reminder for my family and for everybody else, now and for generations to come—a reminder of what happened to us and what could happen again.[5]

Glas-Larsson's post-Theresienstadt and post-Auschwitz experiences include dealing with the loss of a child, whom she had taken into her care in Auschwitz, coping with estrangement from her husband, his suicide when he was forty-two, and the collapse of her second marriage to a Swedish journalist. As her story unfolds the person who emerges is a tired and wise woman, who has allowed suffering to refine her rather than embitter her.

Gerty Spies perceives the post-Theresienstadt experience in terms of both a burden and a summons. She articulates the former in terms of a paradox.

Resonance

It's odd
And strangely sad to me
That prison's rod
Made me feel free.

The chains lie now
At my feet and I am free
But now I know
How heavy freedom weighs on me.[6]

The summons comes to her during moments of stillness and expectancy. It is a call to write.

When the nights are long or when music unlocks my heart, when the breath of spring blows away the boundaries of time, when the

5. Ibid.
6. Original in Yad Vashem.

first stars appear in the evening sky, during such moments it seems as if they had not died, that they are standing close to me. Then it feels as though they are walking beside me or touching my cheek. My friend Martha seems to be looking for me the most. Then for days I go around like a stranger with a floating sensation that a spirit has put a pen in my hand, in order that the bridge between our world and the world of the dead will not collapse under the storms of time.[7]

No poet has built so strong nor so lyrical a bridge to Theresienstadt's dead as Ilse Blumenthal-Weiss. She wrote two volumes of poetry after her liberation—*Das Schlüsselwunder*, published in 1954, and *Mahnmal*, published in 1960. I have chosen, however, to focus on *Ohnesarg* (literally 'without a coffin'), her last book of verse, published in 1984, just three years before her death (the poems are printed in German in Appendix B). It embodies an appropriate commentary on this anthology and offers beyond Theresienstadt a carefully crafted reflection on the Holocaust. The poems translated here fall into four thematic groupings and are undergirded by a common sense of loss. *Ohnesarg* is also a poetic elucidation of loss and on that level functions as the articulation of collective suffering. It is a powerful threnody, a poignant lament about loss, the loss of dignity, of an identity, of a homeland, of language. German continued to be Blumenthal-Weiss's primary language in her American exile but she recognized that in some sense it no longer belonged to her. She mourns that loss in 'Exile':

Exile

My belongings are
The past,
The passing cloud
And the burning bush.

My belongings are
The dimmed wick,
The heap of ice
That stands in front of
House and door.

My belongings are a land
Where I no more belong,

---

7. *Drei Jahre Theresienstadt*, p. 96.

A language that
No more belongs to me.

In one group of poems Blumenthal-Weiss describes the legacy she
has inherited in images that are either insubstantial or invisible—
ash heroes, wind-coffins, coffins made of sighs:

Inheritance

We the offspring,
Siblings to ash-heroes,
Washed ashore
In wind and weather-coffins.
Inheritors of the stake
Dictated to milestones
And redundant gravediggers. . . .
The future, phantom-like, waits on us.

Description

Houses of mist.
Dreams of reality,
Built into the brightest day.

Scaffolds made to fall.
Black signs in Spring.
No earlier. No later.
One must adapt.

Survey

We are offspring,
Caretakers of ash-heroes
Laid out in coffins of the eye,
Crafted from sighs and sorrows.

Tears, the homeless
In the poorhouse of the heart,
Are watering the stake
And the labyrinth of road signs.

Put memory in chains.
Put 'then' and 'never' in chains. . . .
Chains melt like wax.

Loss is also expressed in images of aimless peregrinations on streets that suggest an urban setting, reflecting no doubt Blumenthal-Weiss's own New York exile but also reminiscent of the Expressionist setting, especially the poem 'At Night' with its apochryphal innuendos. The Expressionist 'Schrei' (scream) has become transmuted here into palpable pain:

At Night

At night to wake up
And with darkened houses
Wander through the streets.

To watch an old man
Exchange his crutches
For a ladder to heaven.

To unmask backgrounds
And with the moon-spectator
Carry on whispered conversations.

The day is past and gone.
Silence appeases the cry.
The pain content has turned pale.

In Blumenthal-Weiss's dark, urban streets we see the shadow of Grete Salus wandering through Prague, in Jean Amery's extended hand the hands of the women of the Swiss transport who took their marble memorials to the dead. The predominant tone in these poems is one not of bitterness but of enormous sadness.

Germany-Visit

1.
Cities with new faces
Exchange their ruins for high-rises.
Unconquered overcoming spreads
Out its cloth of forgetfulness.
Groups of people mass around
Pell-mell shop windows,
Gaze in wonder into neon-glare,
Past their conscience.

2.
The neighbour can't read yesterday,
The year that wore mourning.

Swears; had no part in it,
Either with heart or hand.

3.
Coming and going and round and round.
A monument somewhere feigns regret.
Marble pride beams forgotten names.
An old address book laughs at those searching.

4.
The seasons slide through death and life.
Grasp what's long-since gone like jewels
And the golden garment of childhood.—
I had once a lovely homeland.

5.
But in the chimney vaults still chars
Sweet mirth of innocent children.
Still today the blows of fist and club
Chase cradle-song and healing sleep.
Blue sky conceals destruction.
Language forgets the welcome greeting.—
I still can only give as gifts my tears
Since I have seen again the land that once was mine.

Everyday-Citizen

Mauthausen. Auschwitz. Gas.

When the skeleton slips across the square,
Past the guarded graveyard,
Hintz and Kuntz fill up their pipes.
The day tastes like long ago.
We are well.

Mauthausen. Auschwitz. Gas.

Reconstruction

Old house
No longer stands.
New house stands there.
With the built-in yesterday.
With the crimson stripes,
That efface with fresh chalk
And mortar like wounds.

Old house
No longer stands.
New house stands there.
Names on plates with brassy brightness
Guarantee to-morrow
Gushing bright.

During an interview in which the themes of her work were being discussed, Blumenthal-Weiss was asked whether she perceived herself as a witness to a past with which she still had not come to terms. She replied: 'Whenever I write a poem and want to write about the sun, the night keeps coming through.'[8] Her desire and willingness to write about the sun is expressed in tentative rays of light that burst into her verse with all the insistence of life, but they are quickly submerged under great shafts of darkness.

It Happened That

Wanted to go outside.
Smoke met me.
Wanted to see the sky.
Knives and tongs struck me.

Read in books
About joy and woe.
Have seen for myself
What man can do.

At other times she is poised to celebrate but the gesture is aborted in the realization that it was only a dream.

Sometimes

Sometimes.
In a dream
Glories proclaim
The foundling's new fortune.
Sometimes.
In a dream.
Before awakening.

One of the brightest rays of light is found in the poem 'To Take to the Road', largely because of the bold assertion 'Never again'.

8. *Ohnesarg*, p. 76.

To Take to the Roads

To take to the roads.
To take in the blades of
Memory of departed days.
The door, that shut
Stands open,
Bids shooting stars come in,
And rainbows,
Companions of the road.

A voice makes clear:
Never again.
Releases love's word, a blessing
With confessing lips. . . .

As if an angel spoke to me.

In 'Stargreeting' Blumenthal-Weiss projects her suffering on to a seascape and, by releasing her suffering as a barge filled with pain, briefly celebrates rest.

Stargreeting

Falls, sinks into
The glowworm's garden
The stargreeting's
Good night.
Covers up the freight of suffering.
Casts out the nets of dream.
Broods over the Amen's loud ring.

Without memory
Sleep falls into the world.

The poems in which the night alone comes through are the most documentary. Gert Niers makes the pertinent observation that when Ilse Blumenthal-Weiss's poetry is at its most documentary, it is also at its least poetic. The more poetic Nelly Sachs's verse is, he continues, the less it is documentary.[9] Ilse Blumenthal-Weiss's poetic diction is closer to Paul Celan's than it is to Sachs's, particularly in those poems that deal directly with the camp experience

---

9. Gert Niers, *Frauen schreiben im Exil*, p. 104.

where her vocabulary is the explicit language of the camps—bread-rations, uniforms, transports, the Yellow Star, mass graves, gas.

Non-Time

Documents survive
But nobody asks for them;
The yellow star
With the black engraving JEW.
Newsflash:
Shot while fleeing.
Beating on the door.
Uniforms parade.
And in the open field music lashes out.

No bloodshed.
Bloodless torture
Keeps shadow-step to mass-grave.
Hourless time and nameless ones
DEATH.

Loss of dignity is exemplified in its crudest form by mass graves, expressed in the poem 'Everywhere' by the paradox of intimacy and a common grave. In the plaintive last line Blumenthal-Weiss is placing the 'surviving dead' in our hands.

Everywhere

Bedded down together,
Embraced
By a mind-baffling number.
In the noise of cities,
In the meadow- and desert-land,
Here. There. Over there
The surviving dead
In our imploring hands.

In 'Free from Coffin' she resorts to a coined word, characteristic of her poetics in general, to express her outrage:

Free from Coffin

In the grave of free-from-coffin
You can find no gradings.
In the pit called free-from-coffin

Whimpers, cries for help and moanings.
In the grave of free-from-coffin
No flower grows, no blade of grass.
In the pit of free-from-coffin
Smoulders smoke of dead en masse.
In the grave of free-from-coffin
Its light no dawn can share.
In the pit of free-from-coffin
Silent death is groaning there.

In 'Figures' we are given an insight into the inconsolable grief of mourning over a mass grave, of attempting to give individuality to a loved one buried among hundreds, thousands, millions of the dead.

Figures

A hundred. A thousand. A million.
In the figure grave lies the individual corpse.
Now you can choose.
Which number is yours?
When your hearts screams.
When your tears
Want to free from a mass number
That someone,
The dead one
Who belongs to you,
Then only earth and sky
Show you the way.

Tomb of numbers. Places of the dead.
Sepulchre of numbers. Vault of words:
A hundred. A thousand. A million.

As specific as this camp vocabulary is, there is also a sense in which Blumenthal-Weiss's verse is marked by the unspecific. This is particularly apparent in poems that refer to time in a general sense—days, weeks, months, the calendar.

Passing Time

Entries recorded
To no-answer questions
Across the pages of the diary.
After years letting no answer

> Fill up the empty page
> And then years beyond those
> Crossing out with a three-colour pen
> For no one knows what this really is.

This vague, unspecific rendering of time has the effect of injecting into her poetry an overwhelming sense of fatigue and the realization that the pain will never end. Pervasive weariness is also captured in her verse by laconic responses to endless questions that have no answer.

Ohnesarg is essentially genderless and anonymous, with the exception of the poem 'Jean Amery', in which the post-Holocaust suicide of the Austrian philosopher-writer is portrayed as the solution to 'the sufferings of survival':

> *For Jean Amery*
>
> Courage. No fear.
> Hand extended high
> And to that certainty, death,
> Say, pill by pill, welcome!
>
> To see the sky.
> The fresh-made bed
> In the white blossom of last hour.
>
> Breathe. Breathe deep.
> Breathe out death's final consolation
> Into dream of twilight sleep.
>
> Auschwitz and Buchenwald.
> The suffering of survival all done.
> Darkness yields to light.

Yet genderless and nameless as most of these poems are, there resonates between their lines voices of the women of Theresienstadt. In Blumenthal-Weiss's dark, urban streets we see the shadow of Grete Salus wandering through Prague, in Jean Amery's extended hand the hands of the women of the Swiss transport who took their lives. Somehow, we also better understand Gerty Spies's decision to remain in Germany. Hedwig Ems's inability to articulate her loss has surely found a home in these poems.

Epilogue

In the summer of 1987, after working on the Theresienstadt files at the Yad Vashem in Jerusalem, my destination and, in a sense, the terminus of my three-year research was Terezin.

The presence of some soldiers in the quiet, drab streets was the only indication that Terezin was once more a garrison town. Earlier in the day I had visited the Little Fortress a few miles away and along with dozens of tourists, mostly from the Eastern Bloc countries, had been given a guided tour of the barracks and courtyards. Each block, cell and courtyard was carefully marked. The exhibits were as tastefully displayed as any Holocaust exhibit I have seen and correctly stressed the political history of the Little Fortress. Posters highlighted the resistance of a group of Communist youths against imperialism. That too was correct. I remembered that they had been shot in one of the courtyards for their political activities. But when I asked about Terezin my informant told me that Terezin was the Jewish ghetto a few miles away and warned me not to take any photographs there, for it was a military town.

In Terezin there are no signposts or markings to indicate where thousands of Jews once lived and worked. The only sign that they had been there at all was the well-kept cemetery where thousands of gravestones have been erected to the dead of Theresienstadt. Flags representing their country of origin flank the grounds.

Had I not been familiar with the plan of Theresienstadt it would have been difficult to determine which building had been the women's barracks, which the administration building, etc. My main impression of Terezin is that it is a town that is off-limits. When I inquired in German at the hotel about the availability of a room the man in the office did not look up from assiduously drawing lines into an office ledger. He responded in German to my second inquiry by gruffly telling me to wait. Since the page was only half-full I left and headed out of town, along the same road that Grete Salus had walked back to Theresienstadt, heading in the same direction northwards that Gerty Spies had longed to look.

Terezin, once a sluice, is now a ghost-town with a past that is not worth signposting. Had the women represented in this book not written these memoirs and poems, a large portion of its three-and-a-half-year history as Theresienstadt would have remained un-marked, hidden behind the ramparts of Terezin.

Self-Portrait

With death as my shawl
I wander behind footprints
And the echo of
Years ago. Years ago.
Stand on ocean shore of tears
And ignite the memorial candle.

Ilse Blumethal-Weiss[1]

---

1. *Ohnesarg*, p. 66.

Bibliography

AARON, FRIEDA W., 'Poetry in the Holocaust: Ghetto and Concentration Camp Poetry'. Dissertation. City College of New York, 1985.

ADLER, H. G., *Theresienstadt 1941–1945. Das Antlitz einer Zwangsgemeinschaft.* Tübingen: Mohr, 2nd edn 1960.

ADORNO,T. W., 'Engagement', *Noten zur Literatur* III. Frankfurt-am-Main: Suhrkamp, 1965.

ALEXANDER, EDWARD, *The Resonance of Dust: Essays on Holocaust Literature and Jewish Fate.* Columbus: Ohio State University Press, 1979.

ANDERS, BERTA, 'Berta Anders ist tot', in *Ich geb Dir einen Mantel*, ed. Berger *et al.*

AUERBACHER, INGE, *I am a Star: Child of the Holocaust.* New York: Prentice-Hall, 1986.

BERGER, KARIN, HOLZINGER, ELISABETH, PODGORNIK, LOTTE, and TRALLORI, LISBETH N., eds., *Ich geb Dir einen Mantel, daß Du ihn noch in Freiheit tragen kannst: Widerstehen im KZ. Österreichische Frauen erzählen.* Vienna: Promedia Druck und Verlagsgesellschaft m. b. H., 1987.

BLOEMENDHAL, ALICE, 'Theresienstadt einmal anders'. Jerusalem: Yad Vashem Archives, n.d. 02/452.

BLUMENTHAL-WEISS, ILSE, *Das Schlüsselwunder.* Zürich: Classenverlag, 1954.

——, 'Das war Theresienstadt', *Aufbau*. 1960.

——, *Ohnesarg.* Hanover: Postkriptum Verlag, 1984.

——, *Mahnmal.* Darmstadt: Luchterhand Verlag, 1960.

——, *Begegnungen mit Else Lasker-Schüler, Nelly Sachs Martin Buber.* Privately printed for the Leo Baeck Institute, New York, 1977.

BOR, JOSEPH, *The Terezin Requiem*, trans. E. Pargeter. New York: Knopf, 1963.

BRESLAUER, KÄTHE, 'Erinnerungen an Theresienstadt'. Jerusalem: Yad Vashem Archives, n.d. 02/217.

CARO, KLARA, Unpublished material. Jerusalem: Yad Vashem Archives, 1946. 02/244.

CERNYAK-SPATZ, SUSAN E., *German Holocaust Literature.* New York: Lang, 1985.

CONSTANZA, MARY S., *The Living Witness: Art in the Concentration Camps and Ghettos.* New York: Free Press, 1982.

DORMITZER, ELSE, 'Die Kristallnacht'. Jerusalem: Yad Vashem Archives, n.d. 02/139.

——, 'Erlebnisse in Nürnberg'. Jerusalem: Yad Vashem Archives, 1947, 02/53.

——, 'Leben in Theresienstadt'. Jerusalem: Yad Vashem Archives, 1945, 02/392.

——, *Theresienstädter Bilder.* Hilversum: De Boekenvriend, 1945.

EHRMANN, FRANTISEK, HEITLINGER, OTTA and ILTIS, RUDOLF, eds., *Terezin*. Prague: Council of Jewish Communities in Czech Lands, 1965.

EISENKRAFT, CLARA, *Damals in Theresienstadt*. Wuppertal: Aussaat Verlag, 1977.

EMS, HEDWIG, unpublished material. Jerusalem: Yad Vashem Archives, 1947. 02/241.

FLEMING, GERALD, *Hitler and the Final Solution*. Berkeley, Calif.: University of California Press, 1982.

FRAHM, PAULA, 'Theresienstadt von einer Blinden erlebt und niedergeschrieben'. Jerusalem: Yad Vashem Archives, n.d. 02/575.

GILBERT, MARTIN, *The Holocaust*. New York: Hill & Wang, 1978.

GLAS-LARSSON, MARGARETA, *Ich will Reden: Tragik und Banalität des Überlebens in Theresienstadt und Auschwitz*. Vienna: Fritz Molden, 1981.

GREEN, GERALD, *The Artists of Terezin*. New York: Hawthorne Books, 1969.

GROAG, TRUDE, 'Namen und Ortschaften in Erinnerungen der Frau Trude Groag'. Jerusalem: Yad Vashem Archives, n.d. 03/3938.

GROLL, GUNTER, *De Profundis: Deutsche Lyrik in dieser Zeit: Eine Anthologie aus Zwölf Jahren*. Munich: Desch Verlag, 1946.

HEINEMANN, MARLENE E., *Gender and Destiny: Women Writers and the Holocaust*. Westport, Conn.: Greenwood Press, 1986.

HERSKOWITZ, EVA, Unpublished material. Jerusalem: Yad Vashem Archives, n.d. 02/365.

HILBERG, RAUL, ed., *Documents of Destruction: Germany and Jewry 1933–1945*. Chicago, Ill.: Quadrangle Books, 1971.

JACOBSOHN, JACOB, The Daily Life, 1943–1945. London, 1946: Yad Vashem Archives.

——, 'Von Berlin nach Theresienstadt'. Jerusalem: Yad Vashem Archives, n.d. 02/373.

KARAS, JOSEPH, *Music in Terezin*. New York: Leo Baeck Institute, n.d.

KATZ, ESTHER and RINGELHEIM, JOAN MIRIAM, eds., *Women Surviving the Holocaust*. New York: Institute for Research in History, 1983.

KOLMAR, GERTRUDE, *Dark Soliloquy*, trans. Henry A. Smith. New York: Seabury Press, 1975.

KRAMER, EDITH, 'As a Doctor in Theresienstadt'. New York: Leo Baeck Institute, n.d.

——, 'Hell and Rebirth'. New York: Leo Baeck Institute, 1977.

KRAMPEL, REGINE, New York: Leo Baeck Institute, 1943.

LASKA, VERA, ed., *Women in the Resistance and in the Holocaust: The Voices of Eyewitnesses*. Westport, Conn.: Greenwood Press, 1983.

LEDERER, ZDENEK, *Ghetto Theresienstadt*. New York: Fertig, 1983.

LIPMAN, ERIC, 'A Trip to Ghetto Theresienstadt'. New York: Leo Baeck Institute, 1973.

LUSTIG, ARNOLD, *Diamonds in the Night*, trans. G. Theiner. London: Hutchinson, 1962.

——, *Night and Hope*, trans I. Urwin. Prague: Artia, 1962.

MARX, HENRY, 'Im Angesicht des Todes', *Aufbau*, 1986.

MIGDAL, ULRIKE, *Und die Musik spielt dazu: Chansons und Satiren aus dem KZ Theresienstadt*. Munich: Piper, 1986.

MURMELSTEIN, RABBI DR BENJAMIN, Ansprache gehalten zur Begrüssung der Vertreter des Internationalen Roten Kreuzes in Theresienstadt durch den Judenältesten Dr. Murmelstein. Jerusalem: Yad Vashem Archives, 1945. 02/505.

NIERS, GERT, *Frauen schreiben im Exil. Zum Werk der nach Amerika emigrierten Lyrikerinnen Margarethe Kollisch, Ilse Blumenthal-Weiss, Vera Lachmann.* Frankfurt, Berne and New York: Peter Langer Verlag, 1988.

OESTREICHER, ELSA, 'An Annchen'. New York: Leo Baeck Institute, 1957.

PRESSER, JACOB, *The Destruction of the Dutch Jews.* New York: Dutton, 1969.

ROSENFELD, ALVIN H., *A Double Dying: Reflections on Holocaust Literature.* Bloomington, Ind.: Indiana University Press, 1980.

ROSKIES, DAVID G., *Against the Apocalypse.* Cambridge, Mass.: Harvard University Press, 1984.

SALOMON, ROSA, Erlebnisse einer Achtzigjährigen im KZ Theresienstadt. New York: Leo Baeck Institute, n.d. 636.

SALUS, GRETE, *Eine Frau erzählt.* Bonn: Kolten, 1958.

SCHLÖSSER, MANFRED, ed., *An den Wind geschrieben: Lyrik der Freiheit 1933–1945.* Darmstadt: Agora, 1961.

SCHMAHL-WOLF, GRETE, *Sterben.* New York: Leo Baeck Institute, n.d. 069/72.

——, [Untitled] New York: Leo Baeck Institute, n.d. 069/72

SINGTON, FRIEDA, Unpublished material. Jerusalem: Yad Vashem Archives, n.d. 02/214.

SPIES, GERTY, *Drei Jahre Theresienstadt.* Munich: Chr. Kaiser Verlag, 1984.

——, 'Tagebuchfragment aus Theresienstadt'. Jerusalem: Yad Vashem Archives, n.d. 02/69.

STAMM, ANNA, *Streiflichter aus dem KZ Theresienstadt.* New York: Leo Baeck Institute, April 1970.

STARKE, KÄTHE, *Der Führer schenkt den Juden eine Stadt.* Berlin: Haude & Spenersche Verlagsbuchhandlung, 1975.

STEINHAUSER, MARY, and Dokumentationsarchiv des oesterreichischen Widerstandes, eds., *Totenbuch Theresienstadt: Damit Sie nicht vergessen werden.* Vienna: Junius Verlags- und Vertriebsgesellschaft m. b. H., 1987.

STERNBERG, ALEXANDRA, Unpublished material. Jerusalem: Yad Vashem Archives, n.d. 02/240.

STRACH, ADELE, *Einmal und Jetzt.* New York: Leo Baeck Institute, n.d. 069/77.

VOLAVKOVA, H., ed., *I Never Saw Another Butterfly.* New York: McGraw Hill, 1964.

WEBER, ILSE, Unpublished material. Jerusalem: Yad Vashem Archives, n.d. 05/271.

WEINBERG, WERNER, *Self-Portrait of a Holocaust Survivor.* Jefferson, NC: McFarland, 1985.

WOLFENSTEIN, MINA, Unpublished material, New York: Leo Baeck Institute, n.d. 064/78.

WYMAN, DAVID S., *The Abandonment of the Jews: America and the Holocaust 1941–1945.* New York: Pantheon Books, 1985.

Appendix A

The Poems of Else Dormitzer

Vorwort

Euch, meine Schicksalsgenossen von Theresienstadt, sei dies Büchlein gewidmet![1] So oft ich Euch diese Verse vorlas, ertönte ringsum der Ruf: 'Die Gedichte müssen Sie drucken lassen, wenn wir erst frei sind!' Ich versprach es! Nun sind wir frei und ich löse mein Wort ein.

Erinnerungen steigen in mir auf an die mit Euch gemeinsam verlebte schwere Zeit, da Hunger und Elend, Qualen mannigfachster Art das Dasein unerträglich machten, der Tod uns als Erlöser erscheinen musste. Solch gemeinschaftliches Erleben bindet fester als Blutsverwandtschaft, als jarzehntelange Freundschaft von Jugend an.

Im Sinne dieser Verbundenheit weihe ich Euch die "Theresienstädter Bilder."

Hilversum (Holland) im Herbst 1945
Else Dormitzer

Volkszählung (pp. 80–2)

Im Morgengrau'n durchziehen dichte Massen
Theresienstadts sonst menschenleere Gassen,
In Fünferreih'n sieht man in langen Zügen
Sie um die Plätze und die Ecken biegen,
Der Ordnungsdienst sieht nach, ob keiner fehlt—
Das auserwählte Volk wird heut' gezählt!

1. The poems 'Theresienstadt Pictures' were written in Theresienstadt between 1943 and 1945. After Dormitzer's release and return to Holland they were printed by De Buekenvriend Press in Hilversum, in a limited edition of 500 copies. The first fifty appeared in special editions and bear the signature of the author. Otto Treurmand designed the cover. The poems were printed in Dutch medieval script by J. K. Smit & Sons Press Amsterdam. This Foreword translates as: 'To you, my companions of fate of Theresienstadt, I dedicate this little book! Whenever I used to read these poems to you the resounding cry was, 'You must publish these poems as soon as we are free again'. I promised! Now we are free and I am keeping my word. Memories arise in me of the hard times we spent together when hunger, misery and tortures of one kind and another made life intolerable, when death inevitably seemed more like our rescuer. Experiences like these shared together bind more firmly than blood relationships and life-long friendships. With this relationship in mind I dedicate to you the 'Pictures of Theresienstadt'.

Man kann erblicken jede Art von Typen,
Denn nur die Kranken sind zurückgeblieben,
Man hat sie alle mit vereinter Kraft
Um 5 Uhr früh in's Siechenheim geschafft,
Der Lahme führt den Blinden, der sich quält —
Das auserwählte Volk wird heut' gezählt!

Gar viele Mütter schieben Kinderwagen,
Der Vater muss sein krankes Söhnchen tragen,
An Krücken, Stöcken schleppen sich die Alten,
Der Zählerdienst beginnt mit seinem Walten.
Aus Wolken sich die bleiche Sonne schält —
Das auserwählte Volk wird heut' gezählt!

Nun ist das Ziel erreicht' in weitem Bogen
Wird in den Bauschowitzer Grund gezogen,
Kein Stuhl, kein Stein und keine Bank zum Sitzen,
Kein Mäuerchen, den Rücken nur zu stützen,
'In Hundertschaften steh'n!' heisst der Befehl,
Damit das auserwählte Volk man leichter zähl'!

Der Mundvorrat ist aus, er war bescheiden,
Der Hunger wühlet in den Eingeweiden,
Nichts Warmes wird gereicht, kein Tropfen Wasser
Und Vieler Antlitz wird nun blass und blasser.
Wie hart, wenn Frost mit Mangel sich vermählt —
Das auserwählte Volk wird heut' gezählt!

Und Stund' um Stund' verrinnt! Auf hartem Raine
Sitzt, wem versagen Rücken, Herz und Beine!
So Mancher fühlt sich schwach und schwächer werden
Und sinkt bewusstlos nieder auf die Erden,
Dort liegt er ausgestreckt, als wie entseelt —
das auserwählte Volk wird heut' gezählt!

Die Nacht bricht an, kein Stern am Firmament!
Auf allen Lippen eine Frage brennt:
'Wird man hier blieben bis zum frühen Morgen?'
Welch Zittern, Zagen, Bangen, welche Sorgen!
Verzagt selbst der, den sonst sein Glaube stählt —
Das auserwählte Volk wird heut' gezählt!

Doch endlich kommt die Kunde — welches Glück!
'Der Jude darf in's Ghetto jetzt zurück!'
Ein Hasten, Schieben, Drängen, Stossen, Fluchen,
Die Elteren Kinder, Kinder Eltern suchen.
Dann geht's rach Haus und keiner sich verhehlt:
Das auserwählte Volk ward heut' gezählt!

Verlorene Jahre (p.113)

Wer gibt uns die verlor'nen Jahre wieder,
In denen unsre Seele zagend bangte,

Das Herz nach Euch, Ihr Lieben, heiss verlangte.
Wo seid Ihr, Kinder, Eltern, Schwestern, Brüder?

Ihr, die mit uns in innigem Verbande
Zusammen lebten, bis ein hart' Geschick
Uns jählings traf, vernichtend alles Glück,
Und Euch wie uns entführt in fremde Lande.

Nicht wissen wir, wo wir Euch suchen sollen,
Kein Gruss von Eurer Hand ward uns gegeben.
Wir fragen angstvoll: 'Seid ihr noch am Leben?'
Und bittre Tränen aus den Augen rollen.

Was gibt uns Kraft, dies alles zu ertragen?
Die Hoffnung, Herr und Gott, auf Dein Erbarmen!
Hilf Deinem Volk, dem unglücksel'gen armen
Und führ' uns bald zu bess'ren, hellen Tagen.

Transport (pp. 88–9)

Ein Raunen, Flüstern, ängstlich' Fragen
In düsteren Dezembertagen,
Hier laute Klag', dort leises Weinen,
Die ganze Stadt ist auf den Beinen,
In aller Mund ein einzig Wort:
    Transport!

Ein eis'ger Wind bläst durch die Gassen,
Zum letzten Mal heisst's: "Brote fassen!"
Ein Wäscheflattern, Betten rollen
Ein Rucksackpacken, Helfenwollen
Der Freunde, eh's zur Schleus' geht fort:
    Transport!

Nun ist's soweit—ein Abschiedsblick,
Ein Händedruck, der Wunsch: Viel Glück!
Mit seiner Sens' steht Einer dort,
Der wanket nicht und geht nicht fort,
Er zieht mit Euch von Ort zu Ort:
    Transport!

Ein Ruf, ein Pfiff—es flattern Dohlen,
Wann wird man wohl die Nächsten holen?
Ist dies Geschick auch uns beschieden?
Wann winkt uns Ruh? Wann gibt es Frieden?
Beschütze uns, Du, unser Hort,
    Vor dem TRANSPORT!

Nachschub (pp. 38–9)

In Eis und Schnee, in Sturm und Regen
Begegnet man auf allen Wegen

Viel ausgemergelten Gestalten,
Die in der Hand den Blechnapf halten.
Sie woll'n—teils offen, meist verstohlen—
Sich Nachschub im Kasernhof holen.
Dort stehen sie in langen Schlangen
Und fragen voller Angst und Bangen:
'Wird es ein wenig Suppe geben?
Wir brauchen nötig sie zum Leben!
Erhält man sie auch ohne Karten?
In jedem Fall heisst's: Warten, warten!'
Man wartet nun in dumpfem Schweigen,
—Wie langsam doch die Stunden schleichen!—
Reibt sich die Hände, streckt die Glieder
Und stampfet, trippelt auf und nieder.
Dazwischen hört man Männer brüllen,
Die, um dem Geltungstrieb zu stillen,
Ihr Aufsichtsamt dazu erwählen,
Die Harrenden noch mehr zu quälen.
Vom Turm schlägt's zwei—die Hoffnung steigt!
Ob sich der Dampftopf endlich zeigt?
Da schallt ein Ruf von Weitem her:
'Es gibt heut keinen Nachschub mehr!'
Der Aufsichtsmann mit grobem Ton
Jagt die Enttäuschten rasch davon;
Die kehren nun mit stierem Blick
In ihre kalte Stub' zurück,
Und ist der nächste Mittag da,
Gehn wieder sie nach Golgatha!

Einst und Jetzt (pp. 56–7)

Einst warst Du so rundlich,
Jetzt bist Du so schlank.
Einst warst kerngesund Du,
Jetzt bist Du meist krank.
Einst warst Du so sorglos,
Jetzt bist Du geplagt.
Einst warst Du voll Mut
Und jetzt bist Du so arm,
Einst warst Du frisch-fröhlich,
Jetzt fehlt jeder Charme.
Einst warst Du ein Gourmand,
Jetzt frisst Du selbst Mist.
Einst warst Du goldehrlich,
Jetzt bist Du ein Dieb,
Einst schätzten Dich alle,
Wer hat Dich jetzt lieb?
Einst halfst Du den Ander'n,
Jetzt sorgst Du für Dich,

Einst warst Du verlässlich
Jetzt lässt Du in Stich.
Einst warst Du voll Güte,
Jetzt bist Du brutal,
Einst schliefest Du köstlich,
Jetzt wachst Du voll Qual.
Einst warst Du so reich
Und jetzt bist Du so arm,
Einst warst Du frisch-fröhlich,
Jetzt fehlt jeder Charme.
Einst warst Du ein 'Jemand',
Jetzt bist Du ein 'Nichts',
Einst warst Du blitzsauber,
Vor Schmutz Du jetzt pichst.
Einst freut' Dich das Leben,
Jetzt hast Du es satt—
Das ist der Erfolg von
Theresienstadt!

Wanzennacht (pp. 42–4)

Es gibt hier Plagen ohne Zahl,
Doch keine schafft uns solche Qual
Wie die der Wanzen, die die Nacht
Zu einer wahren Hölle macht.
Sonst—nach des Tages Last und Müh'—
Begab man sich zu Bette früh
Und dachte (war man auch nicht satt!)
'Jetzt kann mich ganz Theresienstadt . . .'
Man schlief rasch ein, vergass sein Leid
Und träumte von der alten Zeit.
Doch jetzt? Man greift zum Veramon,
Nimmt Sedormit, Pyramidon,
Schluckt eimerweise Quadronox. . . .
Es hilft doch alles nichts, Du Ochs,
Denn pünktlich mit dem Schlage zehn
Musst in den Wanzenkampf Du geh'n.
Ein Jucken, Beissen, Kribbeln, Krabbeln,
Du fühlst die Biester an Dir zappeln,
Und hast Du zwanzig umgebracht,
Ein Heer von Hundert Dich verlacht.
'Was tun?' spricht Zeus—man rennt hinaus
Und schüttelt seine Betten aus.
Ein anderer, des Ekels voll,
Springt in der Stub' herum wie toll;
Der dritte isst verzweifelt Brot,
Sein Nachbar gar mit Selbstmord droht,
Doch keiner, keiner löst die Frag':
'Wie wird man Herr der Wanzenplag'?'

Die Lösung erst dereinst gelingt,
Wenn Frieden uns und Freiheit winkt,
Denn sind wir glücklich erst zu Haus',
Adieu dann Wanze, Floh und Laus!

Glimmer (pp. 47–8)

Um vier Uhr aus dem Bett heraus,
Um fünf Uhr schleunigst aus dem Haus,
In Finsternis auf schlechten Wegen
Eilt man dem gleichen Ziel entgegen.
Da hilft kein Klagen, kein Gewimmer:
Es ruft der Glimmer, Glimmer, Glimmer!

Zweitausend Frauen, jung und alt,
Steh'n in des Frohndienst's Allgewalt,
In langen Schichten von acht Stunden
So werden sie geplagt, geschunden
In schlechter Luft, im engen Zimmer,
Das will der Glimmer, Glimmer, Glimmer!

Auf hartem Schemel ohne Lehn',
Kann man sie rastlos schaffen seh'n,
Der Rücken krumm, im Kreuz ein Schmerz,
Bald rasch, bald langsam schlägt das Herz
Und vor den Augen—welch Geflimmer!
So wirkt der Glimmer, Glimmer, Glimmer!

Fürwahr, die Arbeit ist nicht leicht,
Und wird das Pensum nicht erreicht,
So droht als Sühne neues Leid:
"Ihr habt zwei Stunden Strafarbeit!"
Schreit laut ein Aufsichtsmann, ein grimmer,
Im Ton des Glimmer, Glimmer, Glimmer.

Es fallen Opfer ohne Zahl
Bei dieser Arbeit, dieser Qual;
Man trägt auf Bahren sie davon,
Der Tod, er harret ihrer schon.
Der Armsten letzter Ruf ist immer:
'Verflucht der Glimmer, Glimmer, Glimmer!'

Tod in Theresienstadt (pp. 53–4)

Täglich wird das Antlitz blass und blasser,
Ständig steigt in Bein und Leib das Wasser,
Keuchend geht der Atem, kurz und bang
Und die Nächte, ach, wie sind sie lang,
Endlich ruft der Tod: 'Jetzt ist es aus!'
Und die arme Seele fliegt nach Haus.

Umständ' werden hier nicht viel gemacht,
Schnell die Leich' in Positur gebracht,
Eine Wolldeck' zieht man übers Haupt,
Was vorhanden, wird noch rasch geraubt.
Nach zwei Stunden, ohne Ton und Wort,
Schiebt den Toten man zum "guten Ort."
Zwanzig Kisten stehen dort beisammen,
Wandern tags darauf dann in die Flammen;
Freunde und Verwandte rings im Kreise
Schluchzen bei des Kaddisch's frommer Weise.
Kist' um Kiste wird nun rasch getragen
Zu der letzten Fahrt im Leichenwagen;
Man sieht nach, bis er enteilt dem Blick,
Kehrt im Strassenkot zur Stadt zurück.
Eine Frag' beschäftigt Dich allein:
'Wann werd' ich bei solchem Schub wohl sein?'

Finale (p. 107)

Ein Tag wie alle and'ren, öd und leer,
Im Herzen keinen Funken Hoffnung mehr;
Des Dienstes ewig gleichgestellte Uhr
Durch spärlich Essen unterbrochen nur.
Man geht, wie immer, tief verstimmt zur Ruh'
Und schliesst erschöpft die müden Augen zu.
Am Morgen, ha, ein Wunder ist gesch'n:
Man kann rings fremde Uniformen seh'n,
Die Russen sind's, die uns vom Joch befrei'n,
Man höret lachen, weinen, jauchzen, schrei'n,
Reibt sich die Augen—ist's ein schöner Traum,
Der rasch zerrinnen wird wie Seifenschaum?
Nein, es ist Wirklichkeit! Der Spuk ist aus.
O Glück, o Seligkeit—es geht nach Haus!
Wir steh'n am Anfang einer bess'ren Zeit,
Dir, Ewiger, sei unser Dank geweiht.
Wir preisen Dich mit Herz, Vermögen, Seel',
Du hast erlöset Dein Volk Israel!

Appendix B

The Poems of Ilse Blumenthal-Weiss

(Numbers in brackets indicate the page on which the poem appears in the text.)

Klagelied   [vi]

Ach das ewige Leben der Toten,
In Augensärge gebettet,
Unsichtbar. Grell.

Tränen, die Heimatlosen
Im Armenhaushalt des Herzens
Hüllen den Tag ein.
Monat.
Und Jahr.

Geht vorüber.
Kommt niemehr wieder.
Wir müssen aus der Worte Zuendung fliehen
Und das Gedächtnis in Ketten legen.—

Die Ketten schmelzen wie Wachs.

(*Ohnesarg*, p. 12)

Betrachtung   (p. 10)

. . . .
Nichts geht verloren. Alles bleibt bestehn:
Ein Blatt; ein Flötenspiel; ein Wiedersehn.
Die Kerkerwand; der schale Bodensatz.
Das Mohnfeld neben einem Hafenplatz.

Der Liebe Ruf; der Hand bedachter Trost,
Sie warten, bleiben, werden ausgelost
In Stadten, Scheunen, Spiegelmeeren..
Nichts geht verloren. Alles will gehören.

(*Mahnmal*, p. 33)

Bunter Abend   (p. 86–7)

Der Vorhang steigt: Verwandlung fratzt und Miene
Vor einem heimgesuchten Publikum.
Man tanzt; man singt; man dreht sich auf der Bühne
Und bringt die Schwermut mit Kulissen um.

Man glaubt an Masken, die von Versen leben,
An Mondlicht, das auf nahen Hügeln träumt.
Man läßt sich in ein Niemandsland entschweben,
Von Hoffnung und Erinnern breit umsäumt.

Und sieht nicht mehr, daß alle Bilder Schatten,
Und alle Spieler dichte Schleier dämpfen.
Und daß im Flackerschein von Heldentaten
Die Todgeweihten mit dem Leben kämpfen.

Der Vorhang fällt: auf leeren Bodenplanken
Frißt Ungeziefer Leib und Seele fort.
Und morgen früh, wie Vieh zur Schlachtbank, schwanken
Die aufgerufnen Massen zum Transport.

(Mahnmal, p. 24)

In Memoriam
(Theresienstadt 15.10.1944)   (p. 93)

So haben uns die bangen Scheidestunden
Im dunklen Raum des Abschieds eingeschneit.
Und unsre Augen waren nur noch Wunder.
Und unsre Worte waren Ewigkeit.

So haben wir noch einmal alles Leben
Einander wie zum Trost uns hingeschenkt.
Dann hast du mir den letzten Blick gegeben
Und deine Tränen in mein Herz gesenkt.

Mit deinen Händen, betend wie zum Segen,
Hast du zum letzten Male mich erhellt.—
Nun geh ich ohne dich nur immer dir entgegen.
Und trage deinen Tod hin durch die weite Welt.

(Mahnmal, p. 39)

Transport Abgang   (p. 97)

Ich habe Kinder gesehen, krank und vom Fieber verzehrt.
Sie waren ganz still. Sie haben sich nicht gewehrt.
Man stieß sie in irgendeinen
Dunklen, unreinen
Viehwagen hinein
Und ließ sie allein. . . .
Die Kinderchen . . . ganz allein.

Ich habe Frauen gesehen, krank und wie ohne Gesicht.
Sie waren ganz still. Sie rührten sich nicht.
Man hat sie in irgendeinen
Dunklen, unreinen
Viehwagen getrieben.
Dort sind sie liegengeblieben
In Angst und Grauen,
Die kranken Frauen.

Ich habe Männer gesehen, wie Klumpen zuszmmengeballt.
Sie waren alle viele Jahrtausende alt.
Man stieß sie in irgendeinen
Dunklen, unreinen
Viehwagen zum Transport.—
Nun immerfort
Rollen Räder, Schienen entlang,
Zu Folter und Untergang.

(Mahnmal, p. 25)

Exil   (pp. 118–19)

Was mir gehört,
Ist die Vergangenheit,
Die flüchtige Wolke
Und die Dornbuschglut.

Was mir gehört,
Ist das erloschene Licht,
Der Klumpen Eis
Vor Haus- und Zimmertür.

Was mir gehört,
Das Niemehr-Heimatland
Und eine Sprache,
Die mir nicht gehört.

(Ohnesarg, p. 54)

Erbschaft   (p. 119)

Nachkommen wir,
Geschwister der Aschenhelden,
In Wind- und Wettersärgen
An Land gespült.
Erbschaft der Scheiterhaufen
Diktiert den Meilensteinen

Und arbeitslosen Totengräbern.—
Die Zukunft wartet mit Schemen auf.

(*Ohnesarg*, p. 56)

Beschreibung [p. 119]

Häuser aus Nebel.
Träume aus Wahrheit,
Eingebaut in den hellichten Tag.

Gerüste zum Absturz.
Schwarzzeichen im Frühling.
Kein Früher. Kein Später.
Man muß sich fügen.

(*Ohnesarg*, p. 48)

Übersicht (p. 119)

Nachkommen wir,
Betreuer der Aschenhelden
In Augensärge gebettet,
Gezimmert aus Seufzer und Gram.

Tränen, die Heimatlosen
Im Armenhaushalt des Herzens,
Tränken die Scheiterhaufen
Und der Wegweiser Labyrinth.

Legt das Gedächtnis in Ketten.
Legt Damals und Niemals in Ketten.—
Die Ketten schmelzen wie Wachs.

(*Ohnesarg*, p. 64)

Nachts (p. 119)

In der Nacht aufwachen
Und mit verdunkelten Häusern
Durch Straßen wandern.

Zusehen wie ein alter Mann
Seine Krücken eintauscht
Für eine Himmelsleiter.

Hintergründe entlarven
Und mit dem Zuschauer Mond
Flüstergespräche führen.

Der Tag ist verschollen.
Stille besänftigt den Schrei.
Der Inhalt Schmerz ist verblaßt.

(*Ohnesarg*, p. 41)

Deutschland-Besuch   (pp. 120–1)

1.
Wiedergesichtete Städte
Tauschen Ruinen in Hochhäuser um.
Unbewältigte Bewältigung
Breitet das Tuch des Vergessens aus.
Die Masse Mensch gruppiert sich
Um Schaufenster-Kunterbunt,
Starrt bewundernd in Neonhelle,
Am Gewissen vorbei.

2.
Nachbar kann kein Gestern lesen,
Jahreszahl mit Trauerrand.
Schwört; bin nicht dabei gewesen,
Nicht mit Herz und nicht mit Hand.

3.
Kommen und Gehen und Rundherum.
Irgend ein Denkmal täuscht Reue vor.
Marmorstolz prunkt mit vergessenen Namen.
Ein altes Adreßbuch lacht Suchende aus.

4.
Die Jahreszeit durch Tod und Leben schleifen.
Das Längstvorbei wie ein Juwel ergreifen
Und einer Kindheit Goldgewand.—
Ich hatte einst ein schönes Vaterland.

5.
Noch immer verkohlt in den Schornsteingehäusen
Der Kinder unschuld'ges Lachen.
Noch immer verbannen Faustschlag und Kolben
Das Wiegenlied und den heilenden Schlaf.
Blauer Himmel verschweigt die Zerstörung.
Sprache vergißt den Willkommensgruß.—
Ich habe nur noch Tränen zu verschenken,
Seit ich mein Einstland wiedersehn.

(*Ohnesarg*, p. 58–9)

Bürger-Alltag   (p. 121)

Mauthausen. Auschwitz. Gas.

Wenn das Skelett über den Marktplatz schlürft,
Am behüteten Kirchhof vorbei,
Stopfen Hintz und Kuntz sich die Pfeifen.
Der Alltag schmeckt nach Längstvorbei.
Uns geht es gut.

Mauthausen. Auschwitz. Gas.

(Ohnesarg, p. 65)

Der Neubau   (p. 121)

Altes Haus.
Nicht mehr vorhanden.
Neues Haus steht da.
Mit dem eingebauten Gestern.
Mit den feuerroten Striemen,
Die mit frischem Kalk und Mörtel
Wundenmale ausradieren.

Altes Haus.
Nicht mehr vorhanden.
Neues Haus steht da.
Namensschilder messingblinkbank
Garantieren überschwenglich
Sogenannte neue Zeit.

(Ohnesarg, p. 73)

Es Geschah   (p. 122)

Wollte ins Freie gehn.
Hat mich Rauch empfangen.
Wollte den Himmel sehn.
Griffen mich Messer und Zangen.

Habe in Büchern gelesen
Von Freude und Leid.
Bin Zeuge gewesen
Der Unmenschlichkeit.

(Ohnesarg, p. 69)

Manchmal   (p. 122)

Manchmal.
Im Traum
Verkünden Herrlichkeiten
Die Ankunft des Findlings Glück.
Manchmal.
Im Traum.
Vor dem Erwachen.

(*Ohnesarg*, p. 42)

Eine Wanderschaft   (p. 123)

Wandern. Auf Wanderschaft.
Die Halme Erinnerung holen
Entschwundene Tage ein.
Tür, die zuschlug,
Steht offen,
Ladet Sternschnuppen ein
Und Regenbogen,
Die Gefährten der Wanderschaft.

Eine Stimme verständigt:
Nie wieder.
Erlöst das Segenswort Liebe
Mit dem Bekenntnis der Lippen.—

Als spräche ein Engel mich an.

(*Ohnesarg*, p. 43)

Sterngruß   (p. 123)

Fällt, fällt herab
In den Glühwürmchengarten
Der Sterngruß
Gute Nacht.
Deckt die Kummerfracht zu.
Wirft die Traumnetze aus.
Hütet den Amenlaut.

Ohne Erinnerung fällt
Schlaf in die Welt.

(*Ohnesarg*, p. 44)

Un-Zeit (p. 124)

Übriggeblieben die Dokumente,
Nach denen keiner mehr fragt:
Der gelbe Stern
Mit der Schwarzaufschrift JUDE.
Die Eilbotennachricht:
Auf der Flucht erschossen.
Schlag an die Tür.
Uniformenparade.
Und auf freiem Felde die Peitschenmusik.

Kein Blutvergießen.
Blutlose Folter
Begleitet Schatten ins Massengrab.
Ohnestunde und Ohnenamen
Tauschen das Leben um in
TOD.

(*Ohnesarg*, p. 55)

Überall (p. 124)

Nebeneinander gebettet,
Umarmt
Von der unausdenkbaren Zahl.
Im Lärm der Städte,
Im Wiesen- und Wüstenland,
Hier. Da. Und dort
Die überlebenden Toten
In unseren flehenden Händen.

(*Ohnesarg*, p. 60)

Ohnesarg (p. 124–5)

In der Grube Ohnesarg
Gibt es keine Stufe.
In der Grube Ohnesarg
Wimmern Hilferufe.
In der Grube Ohnesarg
Wächst kein Gras und Halm.
In der Grube Ohnesarg
Schwelt der Menschrestqualm.
In der Grube Ohnesarg
Glüht kein Morgenrot.
In der Grube Ohnesarg
Stöhnt die Stimle: Tod.

(*Ohnesarg*, p. 10)

Zahlen (p. 125)

Hundert. Tausend. Million.
Im Zahlengrab liegt der Leichnam Mensch.
Jetzt kannst Du wählen.
Welche Ziffer ist Dein?

Wenn Dein Herz schreit.
Wenn Deine Tränen
Den einen,
Deinen Toten
Befreien wollen
Aus der Massenzahl,
Weist Erde nur und Luft
Den Weg Dir an.

Zahlengruft. Die Totenorte.
Zahlenabgrund. Abgrundworte:
Hundert. Tausend. Million.

(*Ohnesarg*, p. 62)

Zeitvertreib (pp. 125–6)

Aus Ohne-Antwort-Fragen
Eintragungen schreiben
In Tagebuchblätter.

Nach Jahren mit einer Antwort
Leere Seiten füllen
Und sie nach Wieder-Jahren
Ausstreichen mit dem Drei-Farben-Stift.
Denn niemand weiß Bescheid.

(*Ohnesarg*, p. 8)

Für Jean Amery (p. 126)

Mut. Furchtloser Mut.
Hand ausstrecken
Und die Gewißheit Tod
Pille um Pille willkommen heißen.

Den Himmel sehen.
Das frischbezogene Bett
Im Blütenweiß der letzten Stunde.

Atmen. Aufatmen.
Des Abschieds Trostminuten
In Halbschlafträume hauchen.

Auschwitz und Buchenwald.
Die Überlebensqual ist ausgelitten.
Das Dunkel leuchtet Licht.

(*Ohnesarg*, p. 37)

Selbstbildnis (p. 128)

Mit dem Tod als Umschlagetuch
Wandere ich hinter Fußspuren her
Und dem Echo
Vor Jahren. Vor Jahren.
Stehe am Ufer der Meere aus Tränen
Und zuende das Jahrzeitlicht an.

(*Ohnesarg*, p. 66)

Finally, and in the hope that it would have pleased her, I give the original German of the poem by Ilse Blumenthal-Weiss's daughter Miriam Merzbacher-Blumenthal quoted in translation on pp. 93–4.

Der Ewige Segne und Behüte Dich!
(In Erinnerung an einen Segensspruch, den Eltern ihrer Tochter sagte, bevor sie sich voneinander verabschiedeten)

Links rechts
Rechts links
Strickt eine Mutter
Ein Kleid für ihr Kind.
Links rechts
Rechts links,
Sie strickt ein blaues Kleid.

Links rechts
Rechts links—
'Der Ewige segne
Und behüte dich.
Der Herr hat gegeben',
Links rechts,
'Der Herr hat genommen',
Rechts links,
'Der Name des Herrn
Sei gelobt.'

Links rechts
Rechts links!
Ein Mädchen
Entwachsen dem blauen Kleide,
Links rechts
Steht gesegnet
Und behütet,
Rechts links . . .
Der Herr hat gegeben
Die Öfen genommen
Eltern und Brüder—
Links rechts
Rechts links!

Links rechts
Rechts links.
O Gott, Dein Name sei gepriesen!
Links rechts
Rechts links.
Verherrlicht und geheiligt
Gepriesen und gelobt.
Links rechts
O Gott
Die Öfen!
Gepriesen Dein Name,
Links rechts
Rechts links.

Index

152